The Good Fight

A Paramedic's Story

The Good Fight
A Paramedic's Story

J. CHRISTOPHER THOMAS

Lulu

The following book contains stories of real-life emergencies and medical procedures. Some content may be unsettling for some readers. Names and some details of events have been altered.

ISBN: 978-1-79483-146-9

This book is dedicated to all of the men and women across the world serving in the EMS profession.

- Contents -

- Introduction -

In the grand scheme of things, the field of Emergency Medical Services (EMS) is still quite young. Unlike the police and fire services, which have been around in some form or another for over a century, EMS as we know it only began to take shape in the latter part of the 20th century.

It wasn't that long ago that if someone needed transported to a hospital they would often get an "ambulance" courtesy of the local funeral home. These transport vehicles were staffed by personnel who had little or no training and simply transported sick or injured persons to the local hospital as quickly as they could with little, if any, treatment provided. This is a far cry from the sophisticated EMS systems of modern day, and the journey from the funeral home ambulance to its modern descendent was not a quick one.

Modern EMS can trace its roots to the 1960s, when the National Academy of Sciences National Research Council released a report called *Accidental Death and Disability: The Neglected Disease of Modern Society*. The report, which came to be known as "the white paper," detailed the number of injuries and deaths occurring on highways across the United States. It also brought to light severe deficiencies that existed regarding the delivery of prehospital emergency medical care and transport. Also included in the document were suggestions meant to improve provider training and ambulance service systems.

The Highway Safety Act of 1966 mandated that all states establish some type of safety program specific for highways, which were regulated by federal standards; these programs were also required to include the provision of emergency services. Ultimately, this led to the U.S. Department of Transportation taking a leadership role in the establishment of EMS systems. To date, on a national level, EMS falls under the purview of the U.S. National Highway Traffic Safety Administration.

Over the next half-century, EMS continued to grow. Training programs became standardized and organizations such as the National Registry of Emergency Medical Technicians (NREMT) and National Association of Emergency Medical Technicians (NAEMT) were founded to support EMS professionals. Multiple levels of prehospital medical providers were established, each capable of providing varying levels of care, from basic life support, or BLS, to advanced life support, or ALS.

Military conflicts like those in Vietnam and Korea made evident the importance of providing prehospital care in a timely manner to those injured on the battlefield. Much of what civilian EMS practices, particularly regarding the treatment of trauma patients, has been adopted from military practice during overseas conflicts; this practice continues with modern day conflicts such as those in Iraq and Afghanistan.

Still, despite the pivotal role that EMS provides to the communities across the country, many citizens do not understand exactly what that role entails. Most people have a general idea of what firefighters and police officers do, but many believe that EMS professionals are simply "ambulance drivers" tasked with the responsibility of picking someone up and taking them to the hospital. In truth, their role is much more vital and complex.

In the transport environment, the entry-level EMS provider is the Emergency Medical Technician, or EMT. The EMT is a BLS-level provider who attends training through a national and/or state-approved training program. These programs are often offered through community colleges, career centers, fire departments, and even some high schools. The length of the course varies but in general is between 150-200 hours in duration.

The EMT student will learn basic concepts of patient assessment and management of medical and traumatic emergencies. Amongst other material, they are taught the basics of airway management, cardiopulmonary resuscitation (CPR), management of traumatic injuries, childbirth, and emergency pharmacology.

The Advanced EMT (AEMT) is the next level on the EMS provider totem pole. The AEMT must first become a certified EMT through the appropriate state and/or national credentialing process before returning to school for another 4-6 months of training. AEMT students are taught additional skills such as placing an intravenous (IV) line and administering certain medications that an EMT cannot.

Lastly, is the paramedic, an advanced life support provider who receives extensive training in advanced patient assessment, advanced airway management, cardiology, pathophysiology, pharmacology, and a slew of medical and traumatic emergencies. The paramedic is trained to perform several invasive skills including some minor surgical procedures. Similar to nursing, there are multiple ways to obtain paramedic training, including: non-degree certification programs, associate-level degree programs, and bachelor-level degree programs. Paramedic students spend hundreds of hours participating in clinical rotations, learning how to assess and treat the patients they will someday be called upon to serve.

Despite the critical role they play, and the high level of care they provide, the average pay rate for an EMS provider in the United States as of this printing is just $33,000, according to the Bureau of Labor Statistics. Additionally, EMS providers often fail to receive the

III

same benefits and recognition that their fellow public safety brothers and sisters in the police and fire services receive. In fact, referring to EMS as "public safety" can at times be met with resistance, as some view EMS as a healthcare service and not a public safety entity.

As a practicing EMS provider for nearly 20 years, I have found varying ways to relieve pent-up stress that accumulates from the day-to-day rigors of my chosen profession. In recent years, I found my social media accounts to be a good medium to utilize to express the difficulties we face. In some cases, I discussed general frustrations that I have with the misunderstanding the public (and others in healthcare professions) has when it comes to our line of work. Other times, I discussed specific calls I have been on to illustrate the types of situations we find ourselves in, day in and day out.

Over time, readers commenting on the posts started making a suggestion that I had never really thought about. They started suggesting that I should write a book.

The thought of writing a book had never really crossed my mind. I've always enjoyed writing. I find it very therapeutic, an easy way to relieve stress. But I've never considered tackling the awesome responsibility of taking the experiences I've lived through during my career and putting them on paper for all to see.

I call it an "awesome responsibility" because in my line of work we deal with *people*, and often it's on the worst day of their lives. Not every ending is a happy one. EMS is full of death and despair. In the course of a shift we can see lives shattered, families broken, and all hope lost.

But EMS is also a field where you can save a life, make a difference, and be the best part of someone's worst day. Taking those experiences and putting them into a book in a tasteful, respectful way is a trying challenge. In fact, the book you are reading is the third version I have written, but it is the version that I feel best paints an honest picture of what we see on the streets every day we go to work.

This book is not just for other EMS professionals or for those who think they might want to pursue a career in EMS, and it's not just for the general public either. It's for everybody! Contained within the following pages are real-life stories of courage and compassion that illustrate what the EMS professionals in your community and across the world do on a daily basis, as they fight to make a difference and save the lives of those they've never met.

Let's start by taking a look at how a simple twist of fate took me from being a high school student pursuing a career in TV and film to where I am today. It's a story that many in the public safety professions share with me, and it all starts with a day so many of us will look at as the day that changed the world forever.

- 1 -

A Simple Twist of Fate

It was as if time had just stopped. I remember it like it was yesterday. I was 17 years old, driving to my part-time job at the local Kmart store, and I was stopped at a traffic light. Eastbound traffic had the green light. I watched as car after car crossed the intersection, turning to the north, when suddenly I noticed a passenger vehicle heading southbound towards that same intersection at a high rate of speed. They were obviously not going to stop.

When I realized the collision was going to happen, I reflexively covered my ears. To this day I'm not sure why I did that, but I do remember doing it. The southbound car - a small, red, four-door passenger vehicle – smashed into the driver's side of a smaller-sized pick-up truck. The red car continued past the intersection before coming to a stop while the white truck rolled to a stop in the opposite direction.

I immediately picked up my phone and called 911. I continued driving towards the store while I talked with the 911 operator. She asked for a location and description of the cars, which I gave her. She then wanted to know if there were any injuries. I didn't know the answer. She thanked me for the information and told me that help was on the way. She took my name and phone number and then ended the call.

That could have easily been the end of it, but something didn't sit right with me. I didn't like not knowing whether or not someone was injured. I quickly did a U-turn and returned to the intersection where the crash had happened.

I parked my car out of the way of the flow of traffic and exited. The pick-up truck, struck on its driver's side, was parked a few feet from me. As I was exiting my car, an older gentleman was exiting the truck.

"Are you okay?" I asked him.

"I think so. Are you an officer?" he replied.

An officer? I'm very clearly a teenager.

"No," I said. "I called 911 and wanted to make sure you guys are alright."

The man was looking over his body from top to bottom, checking for injuries. I didn't see anything obvious. I shifted my attention towards the red car. As I approached, I noticed that the driver's side door was damaged in such a way that it could not be opened. The driver had already attempted to open it. It was a young woman, late teens, early twenties maybe.

"Help is on the way. Are you injured?" I inquired.

Crying, she shook her head to reply. It was then that I could hear the sirens. I looked to the north and saw a fire engine approaching the scene, sounding its loud air horn to encourage drivers to yield to them. The engine came to a stop just behind my car.

As one of the firefighters exited the large apparatus, I approached him to share what information I had. He acknowledged what I had to say and thanked me. I stood back to make room for the professionals.

As I got back into my car to leave the congested area, an additional fire truck arrived on the scene as well as two police cars and an ambulance. I watched for a moment as the first responders quickly went to the patients' sides, assessing them for injury and providing medical treatment. There was something about watching the scene unfold that stirred a sense of clarity inside of me.

I want to do THAT.

*   *   *

Fifteen minutes later, I arrived at the store to work my shift as a cashier. I was still feeling the effects of the adrenaline rush that had swept through me at the accident scene. I don't know why I even had a rush. I didn't really do anything. A call to 911 and a well-being check were the extent of my actions. Still, I could not shake this feeling I was having that the fire service was a career that I seriously wanted to explore.

Until that moment, I had spent the last several years preparing for a career in broadcast journalism. I had taken journalism classes, written for the school newspaper, and helped produce the school's TV news show. Never had I considered a career in the fire service or healthcare; although, I did enjoy watching the medical drama *ER* and the first-responder-focused TV show, *Third Watch*.

I wondered how long this feeling would last. Would it just be a transient thing that would pass in due time, or was I looking at the beginning of something bigger? Only time would tell.

*   *   *

May had come, and my senior year was coming to an end. Not only was my desire to become an emergency responder still present, but it was even stronger than it was when the accident happened the previous summer. Not long after my senior year started, a historic event occurred that solidified my decision to pursue a career in the fire service. That event was 9/11.

I, like most of the world, was glued to the television watching live coverage as the events of that fateful day unfolded. Seeing the firefighters, police officers, and EMS workers rushing towards danger as everyone else fled eliminated any doubt that I had about going forward with my plans to become a firefighter. There was no going back on it now. It was what I wanted to do.

Shortly before high school graduation, I went down to the local volunteer fire department and signed up to become a member. I was incredibly excited to finally get the chance to do what I had been thinking about for the past year.

I was issued fire gear, boots, and a helmet. I also began looking into options for EMT training. The local community college would be doing a course in the fall – I would be there for it. After all, the department that I was joining responded to more medical calls in a year than it did fire calls, and all members were required to be certified EMS providers.

The class was held at the college's airport campus which was about a fifteen minute drive from my house. It was every Tuesday and Thursday at 6pm. I continued working at the store, and my manager there was really good about working around my schedule so I could attend class and my clinical rotations.

The class was comprised of a variety of people with a variety of backgrounds. After five months of going to class, we all gathered on a Saturday to take our examinations for certification. At the time it consisted of a skills test and a written exam – which was actually taken on paper. These days most everything is computerized. Although the tests were intimidating, a combination of having great instructors and a desire to succeed led me to successful completion of all exam components. And with that, I became a certified Emergency Medical Technician.

I wasted no time looking for a job. I sat for my first interview at the local ambulance service when I was 19 years old. It wasn't too long after that, that I received a job offer and began working. All the while, I immediately went back to school to take an Advanced EMT course.

The AEMT level no longer exists in Indiana, where I live, or at least not the version that I took. Being an AEMT back then allowed you to do a few things that an EMT could not: start an IV, check a patient's blood sugar, and do basic cardiac monitoring. The AEMT level today has a scope of practice that is much more expanded.

The ambulance service that I went to work for was a private service not primarily supported by tax dollars, like a municipal service would be. We responded to all 911 calls for an ambulance outside the city limits of the county seat, but we were also responsible for doing non-emergency transports. I didn't even know that was a thing until I started working there.

The non-emergency transports that we completed included taking patients from hospital to hospital, hospital to nursing home, and nursing home to doctor's offices, wound care centers, and dialysis centers. I had never really thought about the fact that there are people out there who are unable to sit up in a car or a wheelchair and would need to be transported in a laying position. Although the "E" in "EMS" stands for "emergency," I quickly learned that there is much more to the profession than adrenaline rushes and blood and guts.

That's not to say that there wasn't plenty of blood and guts to see. My first several months on the job were full of a wide variety of call types. Interestingly, I found that I was more interested in the medical calls than the trauma calls. Maybe it was because trauma felt too easy to me.

From an EMS standpoint, it was pretty simple: if it's bleeding, put pressure on it; if it's broken, splint it; and if they're hurting, treat for pain. Now, obviously there's more to it than that, but when you compare medical problems to trauma problems in EMS, it just seems like you have to use your head more for medical cases.

A lot of conditions have similar symptoms and presentations, and often, as the EMS provider, you'd have to fall back on knowledge, training, and experience to ascertain what was wrong with a patient. This is especially important for paramedics because they are able to administer a large quantity of medications that EMTs are not, and it's very important to be sure about what you're treating before giving certain medications.

I quickly learned that there was a lot of stuff that I did not know. Even after I completed my AEMT training and got certified, I didn't know how much I didn't know.

About a year later, I decided to pursue the next step in my career as an EMS professional: paramedic school. Initially, I chose to pursue a non-degree-granting path. Later, I would go back to school and obtain an associate's degree in paramedic science.

Paramedic school was hard. It was quite possibly the hardest schooling I had been through up to that point in my life. There is so much to learn about the human body, what can go wrong with it, and how to treat patients suffering from medical and traumatic emergencies.

I don't think I've ever studied and prepared for anything as much as I did for my paramedic exam. After having spent thousands of dollars on more than a year straight of training, the last thing I wanted to do was blow the certification exam. When the Saturday came that we would spend going through the exam process, I felt ready for it.

It was a long day, consisting of several skills and scenario stations. Luckily, I passed them all on the first attempt. Only one or two of my classmates had to repeat any of them but fortunately also passed when it was all said and done.

When we were done with the skills and scenarios we then had to sit for the written examination. It was 180 questions that covered thousands of pages and multiple textbooks worth of material. It was daunting to say the least. I spent the next hour and a half or so taking the exam, re-reading question after question and answer after answer, just to make sure I wouldn't miss something. When it was over, I turned in my test booklet and took a deep breath. It was one of those tests that you finish and feel like you did pretty well on but are worried that in actuality you completely bombed it. It would be 4-6 weeks before I would find out.

It was September 13th, my mother's birthday, and I was doing my daily check online at the website for the National Registry of EMTs to determine if I had passed my paramedic licensure exam or not. I had probably been checking two or three times a day for the last two weeks and each time it said the same thing: "results pending." But this time was different. This time when the page loaded, it had the word *passed* in bold print, along with *Certification Level: Paramedic*. It was a very fulfilling moment for me. A lot of hard work, sacrifice, and uncertainty had finally paid off.

That evening when we went out to dinner for my mother's birthday I showed her a print out of the results. As most mothers would be, she was incredibly happy and proud of me.

"Best birthday present I could ever get," she said.

Over the next couple of weeks, I transitioned from the role of an EMT to the role of a paramedic. It required several shifts of "clearing." I would have to ride along with several experienced paramedics, and they would determine if I had what it took to practice paramedicine on my own.

The clearing process was intimidating, but I was confidant in my ability to do the job. I embraced the opportunity to work with so many knowledgeable medics, and they served as excellent preceptors and mentors for me during that process. Sometimes, clearing can take several weeks. The goal is for the new paramedic to get a variety of patients who require advanced life support-level care, and you're pretty much at the mercy of the hand you're dealt when it comes to call types that are dispatched to you.

Luckily for me, I seemed to be a black cloud during that one-week period. In the span of a week I responded to a cardiac arrest, two patients in respiratory failure requiring intubation, an unconscious diabetic, and a patient with a heart arrhythmia, amongst others.

My training apparently paid off, as my preceptors all felt that I performed well and unanimously agreed to sign off on me to practice independently. The charts that I had written for those runs were collected and sent to the medical director for review. He would have the final say. Less than a week later he gave the "ok" and my status was officially changed at work to the level of paramedic (which came with a raise, of course).

Finally. After so much uncertainty and questioning of my future I had finally made it to my end goal. It was time to do what I'd wanted to do for years.

*   *   *

About nine years after I became a licensed paramedic, I began looking into furthering my career. I had always been interested in the prospect of becoming a flight paramedic and working for an air medical service. There had been several occasions over the near-decade that I had been a paramedic when a medical helicopter had been called to one of my scenes to take a gravely injured or ill patient to a hospital capable of providing a higher level of care than our local hospitals could. Watching the process of those calls unfold was intriguing.

An opportunity presented itself in the spring of 2014. The opening was for a location which was a little more than an hour from my home. The drive would be worth it though. I submitted my application and within a couple of days received a phone call to schedule an interview. I was beyond excited to have the chance to pursue the next step in my career.

The interview process was fairly straightforward. It started with a multiple choice test to gauge my knowledge of the pre-hospital and critical care transport fields and was immediately followed by a scenario-based oral interview. I went in ready to blow them out of the water but instead promptly went braindead.

"Working on real patients is less stressful than this," I recall saying to the two administrators performing the interview.

We went through five or six different scenarios. All I had to do was talk my way through them. Getting my brain and tongue to work together was the challenge. I muddled through, and in a little less than an hour we were done. I remember walking out of the building just knowing that I had completely blown it.

There's no way. I don't stand a chance.

I only had to wait until the next day to find out that wasn't the case. I was working on the ambulance and had just taken a patient to the ER. I was finishing up on some paperwork when my phone rang. Sure enough, it was a request for a second interview, and they wanted to do it ASAP! We made arrangements to do the interview via webcam the next day. "Excited" doesn't begin to cover how I was feeling.

The interview the next day went well. I spoke with the base manager and one of the flight nurses as well as the regional manager for the program. The questions asked were the typical "canned questions" you'd expect at any job interview. When we were done, I felt the complete opposite of how I did following the first one. I felt confident that I might actually have a chance. A few days later that feeling proved to be correct; I received a job offer and promptly accepted.

The next several months were very exciting. I did not quit my job working on the ambulance but instead switched to part-time status. The orientation period for the helicopter service was several months and even though I had been in the EMS profession for 12 years at that point, I was surprised by how much I still had to learn. It was so enlightening!

I was taught how to perform new skills and procedures, learned about different medications used in the critical care environment, and was introduced to aviation operations and safety. I was like a kid in a candy store. And for the first time in my career, I began to consider a career change, to nursing.

I had never really considered a career in the nursing field. Several years prior I worked for a few months at the local ER, and at that time they used paramedics as nurses. It was a cheap alternative to hiring RNs because they could get away with paying us a lot less to do pretty much the same thing. I would function just as an RN would when it came to taking care of patients.

Over time, the function of paramedics in the ER changed, and they were utilized more as a tech or nurse's aide. But at the time I worked there it was an opportunity to get a good idea of what nursing care would be like, at least in the ER. And I hated it! The biggest "con" for me was feeling like I was a caged bird with no autonomy.

When you're a paramedic working in the field, it's just you and your partner. You do the assessment, you decide on the treatment. You're working under standing orders from your medical director, but ultimately it's up to you to decide which route to go with a patient. I just couldn't get used to not functioning like that, and after only a few months, I quit the hospital gig.

But that was a long time ago and I was a lot younger. The helicopter service had several nurses who used to be medics; some of them still were and carried two licenses. One of those nurses was a guy named Tim, halfway through his 50s with decades' worth of experience and stories. I once asked him why he decided to go to nursing school.

"You mean besides the increase in pay?" he chuckled. "I just began to realize that I was one back injury away from not being able to work as a paramedic anymore. As a nurse, even if I hurt my back there are jobs that you can do that don't require the physical exertion that being a paramedic does," he explained.

He had a good point. As a paramedic your career options are somewhat limited. You pretty much have the choice of working on an

11

ambulance, in a helicopter, running an EMS service, or teaching. That's about it, and I had already done all of those with the exception of running an ambulance service.

Don't get me wrong, there are plenty of people who work a long and fulfilling career as a paramedic. Not long after I was hired on at the helicopter service, a flight medic from another base retired after putting in decades of service as a paramedic. It can obviously be done, but so many medics are forced to work a great deal of overtime or more than one job to make up for the relatively low pay that is common in the field. And at that point I could see myself spending the rest of my career flying, so why not transition to the role of nurse, do the same job, and get paid thousands of dollars more to do it? Makes sense, right?

As time went on, I returned to school with the goal of becoming a nurse. I had to complete a list of general education courses first. I applied to two separate nursing programs and was excited to have been accepted into each of them. But then something unexpected happened that would change that plan.

A little less than two years after I began my flight job, my base manager was offered a position in upper management. Following several conversations with him and my wife, I decided to apply for the open base manager position. Following the interview process, I was elated to be offered the position. Not only did it come with a nice pay raise, but it was finally an opportunity to make an advancement in my career. However, because of the time commitment involved with the position I decided to put off nursing school.

The management position came with its own assortment of stressors, but it was a challenge that I was looking forward to. It allowed me the opportunity to branch out into surrounding counties, Fire/EMS agencies, and hospitals but it came with attributes that weren't necessarily as flattering; like having to be the supervisor to the group of people that one week before had been your peers. It took some getting used to, but I was up for it. I finally had a plan that was in action and knew that things would only get better.

As time went on, however, changes in my personal life led to the decision to leave the air medical service and begin working full-time again for the ambulance service. There were pros and cons to the decision, but ultimately I had to do what was in the best interest of my family.

*　　*　　*

So, now that you know a little bit about my background, let's get on with what this book is all about.

As you read through the following chapters you will bear witness to events that few people experience in their lives. Some of the stories are humorous, some are strange, some are unbelievable, and some are simply heart-breaking. But, they are all true.

This is what it's like to do this job.

These are the things paramedics and EMTs see and do every day of the week.

This is EMS.

2

Twisted Metal and Shattered Lives

When it comes to traumatic injuries, motor vehicle collisions (MVCs) are definitely at the top of the list of mechanisms of injury. Although many collisions end up being property damage only, there is always the possibility of significant injury to a patient. Most calls involving MVCs are easy to forget about, but there are always a few that stick with you.

*   *   *

August 2004

The smoke billowed so high that we could see it from miles away. The sirens echoed off of the buildings as we sped past them, our ambulance just one of several emergency vehicles in a long line weaving in and out of traffic.

I was just 20 years old and had been working as an EMT for the ambulance service for about five months. We had been requested to assist the local municipal fire department with a multiple vehicle crash on a local highway. Dispatch was reporting multiple patients, some of who were entrapped in their vehicles, possible fatalities, and at least one vehicle fire.

It took us about eight minutes to get to the scene. Incident Command informed us to enter the highway east of the crash and go west in the eastbound lanes. Unfortunately, we didn't get that message until it was too late. We were already heading westbound in the westbound lanes which were gridlocked with stopped traffic. The crash was in the eastbound lanes, but several people in the westbound lanes had stopped, which was causing traffic congestion.

There were no crossovers in the area so the only option was to drive through the grassy median, so that's what we did. As we entered the eastbound lanes and approached the scene, we could see that a few other fire trucks, and at least one other ambulance, were already on scene. From our perspective, it appeared the crash was spread out across a quarter-mile of roadway.

The smoke was coming from an engulfed recreational vehicle, the flames licking the bottom of the plume of smoke as it ascended into the clear blue sky on a warm, late-summer day. I could see another vehicle smashed up against the guardrail. Emergency personnel were already tending to the occupants of that vehicle. Two semis appeared to have been involved in a rear-ending and were off to the side of the road. As we got a little closer, we recognized the dismal truth of that collision...a small truck was crushed between the two semis. No one could survive that.

Just as I was picking up the microphone to ask Incident Command where they needed us, a police officer waived us down, motioning to a vehicle that appeared to be undamaged and was sitting off on the shoulder. We pulled up next to it, and I rolled down my window to speak to the officer.

"What do you have?" I asked.

"Four patients. Two of them are kids. They were in the RV," she said. "The girl seems pretty bad."

I shifted the ambulance into park and jumped out, moving quickly to the Good Samaritan's vehicle where the patients had sought some shelter. The young girl, maybe seven or eight years old, was in the backseat. She was breathing but unconscious. The other child, a boy about six years old, was also in the car but was awake and moving around; he only had a scratch on his arm.

"I'm fine," he said. "Just help my sister."

I hollered at a nearby firefighter and requested that he get me a neck brace (we call them c-collars) so I could stabilize her neck in the event she had an injury. He quickly delivered the collar but had to leave us to help elsewhere.

My partner was doing a quick assessment on the children's grandparents; they were the other patients from the RV. The older gentleman had an avulsion to his right hand. The bleeding was minimal and he was given some gauze to put over the wound. The grandmother was complaining of chest pain and we were uncertain whether or not it was due to an injury or some type of cardiac event triggered by the stress of the incident. Either way, the young girl was the priority at the moment.

I quickly placed the c-collar on her and reassessed her level of consciousness. The only response I could get was when I administered painful stimuli by doing a sternal rub; this resulted in a quiet moan.

This is not good.

We hastily, but carefully, moved her from the backseat of the car and onto a backboard before strapping her securely to the stretcher. As we were loading her into the ambulance, my supervisor, a paramedic, popped his head into the back.

"I'd run her in lights and sirens," he said, after seeing her condition.

Typically, a paramedic would be the one caring for someone in the critical condition that she was in, but he was unavailable to ride with us due to helping with other seriously injured patients at the scene. He helped my partner get the grandparents and the brother secured in the truck and closed the door.

En route to the hospital, the young girl remained unconscious but was breathing adequately. I placed an oxygen mask on her and assessed her vital signs. The grandfather was riding in the front passenger seat, and the grandmother was sitting in what we call our airway seat – a seat located near the head of the stretcher. The brother was sitting next to me on the bench seat. I performed a quick physical assessment on the grandmother and checked her vital signs. Luckily, the transport time to the closest hospital was not long.

We've just got to get them there safely and alive.

When we were about five minutes out from the ER, I called in my radio report. They had already received some patients from the accident, and I let them know that they had four more coming.

We were about two minutes from the ER when suddenly our unconscious patient began projectile vomiting. This was a very ominous sign which supported our theory that she had a significant closed head injury. Her vomit sprayed on to me, my partner, the patient's brother, and the ceiling. We quickly rolled the backboard in an attempt to prevent her from choking on the emesis. I reached for our suction device, called a Yankauer, and worked to clear her airway. By now we were pulling into the ambulance bay at the ER.

Extra hospital staff had come down to the emergency department to help out. Coincidentally, there were several nurses there on their day off for training, so that helped when it came to having extra hands. While other EMS personnel who were already at the hospital helped the grandparents and brother, we unloaded the stretcher and rushed the critical eight year old inside.

When we walked through the sliding doors into the ER, it was like a scene from a disaster movie; very much organized chaos. We were directed to take the patient to Exam 3.

The ER doctor and a couple of nurses met us in the room, listened to our report, helped transfer the backboard to the hospital bed, and began treatment. A medical helicopter was already landing outside and would be transporting her to a children's trauma center.

I had to take a moment and stand back, just watching in awe as everyone in that hospital came together as a team to treat the victims of this catastrophe. This was the first time in the five months that I had been with the company that I had experienced anything like this. It was an amazing feeling that is difficult to describe, but it was exactly why I chose to get into EMS.

*   *   *

April 2005

A few months, later I was working the night shift with another EMT named Jason. Jason and I were not regular partners. In fact, it was the first shift that we had worked together. The first few hours of the shift were pretty uneventful. It was shortly after 9PM when all of that came to an end.

On the south side of our county and response area, a small pick-up truck had been driving at a high rate of speed on a country road. The truck had four young adults inside. Two of them were in the cab of the truck, and the other two were riding in the bed. As the vehicle approached an intersection with a major highway, for unknown reasons, the driver failed to stop for a stop sign. The truck crossed the highway, running off the road and smashed head-on into a concrete wall. Witnesses to the crash quickly called 911.

Jason and I had just finished having dinner and were walking back to our ambulance when we heard one of the medic units being dispatched on the call. There was nothing spectacular about the information in the dispatch. It was put out as a typical "motor vehicle accident with injuries." But within a few moments the tones were set off again and now we were being dispatched. This time, the dispatcher included the information that there were multiple patients on scene.

While we were en route, the fire department arrived at the accident scene and advised us over the radio that they had two unconscious patients and two other patients with serious injuries. Once that information was received, dispatch started additional ambulances. The paramedic unit dispatched just prior to us announced over the radio that they were arriving on the scene. We were about two minutes behind them.

As we came around the last turn on the long stretch of highway, the road was congested with stopped traffic and emergency vehicles. The police were attempting to keep a path open for the incoming ambulances. We pulled up, marked on scene, stepped out of the truck, unloaded the stretcher, and began making our way to the wrecked vehicle.

The paramedic from the unit that had arrived before us was walking back towards his ambulance with a patient on his stretcher. I could see it was a young adult male and they were performing CPR on him.

"Where do you need me, Mike?" I asked.

"I don't know. I've got one in arrest," he responded.

19

His crew had plenty of help from fire department personnel so Jason and I continued to the truck. As we approached, I could see another young male sitting in the bed of the truck, his back against the cab. It would appear there was a large indentation in the body of the cab from where his body had impacted it. He was awake and was obviously in pain. The source of his pain was also obvious. Both of his legs were severely deformed; broken in multiple places.

"Who's next?" I asked the firefighters working the scene.

"This one," said one of them as he motioned to a young adult female they were removing from the cab of the truck.

I stepped around to the side and noted that the young woman was unconscious. Another young woman, covered in blood, was outside of the truck crying hysterically. It was the unconscious woman's sister.

"I think this one needs checked out," suggested Joe, one of the county deputies on scene. "I think she's in shock."

"She's walking and talking," I said. "She waits for the next truck."

Our resources were limited and we were in a situation where the worst patients would have to come first. Some would argue that the first medic unit on scene should not have chosen to work on the driver – the male that was in cardiac arrest – and should have instead declared him deceased and moved on to the next most-critical patient who was still alive: our patient.

The male in the back of the truck, although severely injured, was conscious and alert. He was able to tell us what had happened and also informed us that the unconscious female was initially in the bed of the truck with him. When they struck the concrete wall, the force of the impact threw her through the rear window of the cab. She landed inside the cab on her sister's lap.

Now, her sister was walking around screaming and crying in shock. She was covered in blood from where she had been cut from flying glass. Or perhaps the blood was her sister's. Either way, she was awake, talking, and walking around on her own. At the moment, she was not the priority.

The patient had been removed from the vehicle and secured to a backboard by fire department first responders. She had an oxygen mask in place and a bandage over a cut on her forehead. She was breathing on her own, but she was completely unresponsive.

We secured the backboard to our stretcher and quickly loaded her into the ambulance. The closest hospital was about eight minutes away. That would allow me just enough time to complete a rapid examination, assess her vital signs, and start an IV.

During transport, there was no significant change in her condition. I watched her closely, making sure she did not deteriorate on me. She remained unresponsive. After a quick radio report to the hospital, I checked her vital signs one last time; still normal. The next thing I knew, we were arriving at the hospital.

As we rolled her inside the ER we were directed to take her to Trauma 2. The driver that had been in cardiac arrest was in Trauma 1. As we walked past Trauma 1's doors, I looked inside the room to see that the staff had ceased their resuscitation attempts, and he had been pronounced dead.

We took our patient into the neighboring trauma room, transferred the backboard to the hospital bed, and gave report to the ER physician and nursing staff. A short time later, a medical helicopter arrived to transport her to the regional trauma center, which was about one hour away by ground. She was in need of specialized care that our local hospital was unable to provide.

We never did hear what her outcome was. That's so often the case in EMS. We pick them up, do the best we can in the short time we're with them, and drop them off, oftentimes never knowing what happened to them in the end.

*   *   *

June 2009

It was a warm June evening, and my partner TJ and I had been keeping busy for most of the shift. Summertime tends to coincide with an increase in calls involving traumatic injuries. In fact, summer is often nicknamed "Trauma Season" by those in emergency services, and the season was certainly living up to its name. We had just completed from a call at the hospital when dispatch notified us of a significant MVC involving a train and a passenger vehicle.

We were only about five minutes away from the scene of the crash, but the fire department was even closer. In fact, the railroad crossing where the collision had occurred was literally visible from the front door of the closest firehouse. The responding engine company was on scene in seconds. Unfortunately, within a minute or two of their arrival, they got on the radio to inform us of the grim reality of the situation.

"CPR in progress on one adult female. Also have a female child unresponsive but breathing."

I immediately leaned over, grabbed the microphone, and keyed up.

"Dispatch, Medic 30."

"Go ahead," dispatch replied.

"Let's get another ambulance started, and see if we can get a bird in the air."

"Copy."

The engine company had not advised how old the child was, but I knew that if she was unresponsive then the chances of her having significant internal injuries were decent. My plan was to get a helicopter to land at the scene so we could airlift her to a pediatric trauma center.

We pulled up to the scene and found a large crowd of neighbors had gathered, looking on as fire department personnel were working the crash. TJ and I stepped out of the truck, grabbing our gear and made our way across the large grassy field that the van had rolled across after being struck by the train.

As I approached the van, I could see the feet of one of the firefighters sticking out the side window. The van was on its top and Steve, the firefighter, had crawled inside to assess the unresponsive child.

"What do you got, Steve?" I asked.

"She's out, but she's breathing and has a good pulse."

"Okay, good. How much longer until you get her out?" I asked.

"Just another minute," he replied.

"Okay. I'm going to go check on the other patient."

I stepped around the vehicle to find other members of the fire department performing CPR on an elderly female. We found out later that she was the grandmother of the young girl in the van and had been driving. I immediately noted how pale she was and that her head seemed deformed. I leaned over and felt her head, and it felt as if she had sustained significant skull fractures.

"I'm not touching her," I said to Jon, the firefighter performing CPR. "If you want to keep working her until the other ambulance gets here, that's fine."

"Okay," Jon replied.

At the moment, I was the only paramedic on scene. The only provider capable of providing advanced life support interventions to any of the patients there. In that moment, I had to fall back on the principles of triage: the dead are dead, treat the living. So, I left the EMTs and returned to the young girl just as Steve was getting her out of the vehicle. Jean, a captain on the department, was assisting him.

I was able to take a good look at her, and she did not look well. Her skin was pale and her lips were slightly blue which told me she was not getting enough oxygen. And on top of that, she was completely unconscious. I looked up at TJ who was walking towards me.

"Get set up for a pediatric RSI!" I shouted to him.

It took him a second to process what I said, but then it hit him.

"Fuck!" he shouted before turning and heading back towards the ambulance to get the equipment ready.

His response was understandable. RSI, or Rapid Sequence Intubation, is not a procedure without its risks. The procedure consists of putting your patient into a medically-induced coma to allow the passage of a breathing tube down their trachea. The tricky part is that one of the medications administered to the patient is a paralyzing drug which will stop the patient's breathing. Once the drug is administered, there is only a short window of time to get the tube into the patient's trachea, and failure to do so could easily result in the patient's heart stopping from a lack of oxygen.

I had done the procedure on adults several times throughout my career but had never performed it on a child. I was nervous, but I also knew what had to be done. The child most likely had a closed head injury and quite possibly had lost the reflexes that help to protect her airway. This procedure would allow us definitive airway protection and would also ensure her brain received an adequate supply of oxygen.

Just as we were loading the patient into the back of the ambulance, she stopped breathing. TJ grabbed a bag-valve-mask (BVM), which is used to deliver artificial respirations to a patient whose breathing is inadequate, and began ventilating the patient. I grabbed the equipment necessary to establish an IV and placed one in her right arm.

"How much do you think she weighs?" I asked the others in the ambulance, looking for a second opinion to confirm my estimate.

"Looks like 65 pounds, give or take," Steve suggested.

"I agree," I said before reaching into my medication box, removing the required medications for the procedure.

I would use etomidate to induce sedation and succinylcholine for paralysis. Even though the patient was already unconscious, it's always a good idea to ensure they are well sedated. The last thing you want is for a patient to regain consciousness while paralyzed.

While TJ continued to ventilate the young girl in order to ensure she was receiving oxygen, I proceeded to draw up the required amount of medication to perform the procedure. Once I had the appropriate doses ready, I moved into position at the patient's head and double-checked the equipment I would use to perform the intubation. Pediatric laryngoscope, check. Endotracheal tube (ETT) of appropriate size, check. Syringe to fill the balloon on the ETT, check. Suction ready if needed, check. ETT holder, check. $ETCO_2$ detector, check.

Once everything was ready, I reached over to the IV line and administered the etomidate. Once it was in, I grabbed the syringe with the succinylcholine and administered it. I looked at my watch to make note of the time; SUX normally takes effect pretty quickly.

Sure enough, about 30 seconds after administering the medication, the patient stopped breathing (as expected) and her jaw relaxed. I placed the laryngoscope in her mouth, sweeping her tongue from right to left, leaned down and looked into her mouth, searching for the vocal cords. Luckily, they were not difficult to find. I passed the ETT through the cords, inflated the balloon which creates a seal around the tube, and placed the colormetric $ETCO_2$ detector on the tube. TJ attached the BVM to the detector and delivered a breath.

The $ETCO_2$ turned yellow. Fantastic. The color change to yellow confirmed that the ETT was correctly placed and that carbon dioxide was being detected. I placed a stethoscope over the girl's chest and listened for lung sounds. Lung sounds were present on both sides but were a little diminished on the left. Her oxygen levels remained near 98%-99%, and the rest of her vital signs were stable.

The procedure had gone according to plan. I secured the ETT in place. About a minute or two later, the back doors of the ambulance opened to reveal the flight crew standing ready with their equipment.

While we were performing the intubation, I heard the familiar sound of the helicopter overhead. They landed in a field not far from the ambulance and were given a ride over to our location in one of the fire department's command vehicles.

"Hey, guys," the flight paramedic said. "What do you have?"

I gave a report to the crew about the patient's condition and what we had done to treat her. We assisted in getting her hooked up to their equipment before driving the ambulance over to where their helicopter was located.

After assisting the flight crew with loading the patient into the helicopter, we cleared the landing zone area and watched as the engine spooled and the aircraft lifted from the ground to begin their transport to the children's hospital. I turned and looked at the other responders who had lent a hand treating the patient.

"Good work, guys." I said.

I then redirected my attention towards the accident site. The elderly female's body was now covered with a sheet. The second ambulance had arrived and although the crews tried their best to resuscitate the woman, her injuries were too severe.

Our patient remained stable during the flight. We later found out that she had sustained a skull fracture, a pneumothorax (collapsed lung), and a lacerated spleen. Thankfully, she made a complete recovery and was able to return home to enjoy the remainder of her summer vacation.

Her grandmother was buried a few days after the accident.

3

Innocence Lost

When you do this job long enough, you are sure to have calls that stick with you, and it is almost an absolute guarantee that someone will eventually ask you the dreaded question: "What's the worst thing you've ever seen?"

I've never understood why someone would have the desire to ask anyone to relive the worst thing they've ever seen, but the question is inevitable. Whether it's friends, family members, new co-workers, or complete strangers, someone will eventually ask you. There are a lot of different calls that come to my mind when I get asked that question; however, I never give the person asking the question what they're looking for. Instead, I usually tell them about the obese gentleman that was stuck in a bathtub; that usually leads to a look of disappointment on their face. To be fair though, it was a "traumatic" experience.

The truth, of course, is that I've seen much worse than that – much, much worse. I don't dare say that I've seen the worst there is to see. I know that I haven't, and I sympathize for those who have. But I often joke with staff in the emergency department that they don't see the worst of the worst because those patients never make it to the hospital. They get put into body bags at the scene.

However, sometimes we make it to a call where the patient is still alive or there is a glimmer of hope that they can be saved; or maybe, more realistically, it's just blind optimism. That was probably the case one hot, late summer night, just a few years into my career as a paramedic.

*   *   *

August 2007

My partner and I were sitting in the dayroom at our station watching TV when we heard the tones drop for an emergency call. All these years later, and I still remember the address of the call. I remember every word Sara, the dispatcher, said: "1 year old infant, cardiac arrest." My heart sank. Even though I had been in EMS for nearly 5 years, with the last 2 years as a paramedic, I had not yet been on a resuscitation call involving an infant. My partner and I immediately jumped up and ran towards the ambulance. I can't remember the last time that I actually ran to the ambulance. Honestly, I don't think I ever had. It was 9:25pm.

It seemed like it took forever to get to the scene. Given the time of night, traffic was pretty light, but it still felt like an eternity. We heard the first-responding fire apparatus mark on scene. In the back of my head I kept hoping that someone from the crew would get on the radio and advise us that CPR was <u>not</u> in progress and that the baby was breathing. But that didn't happen.

We arrived on the scene. The house was a quaint little home. Nothing too special. Three bedrooms and a bath. The yard appeared to be taken care of, and there was an older model sedan parked in the driveway. The fire department's rescue truck was parked outside, strobes flashing and red lights turning. I grabbed our pediatric jump bag and started up the walkway to the house. It was like a scene from a TV show or movie – everything felt like it was moving in slow motion.

I entered the house and found a sparsely furnished living room with stains on the floor and a musty odor in the air. I could hear commotion coming from one of the back bedrooms. As I made my way back to the room, I was running everything that needed to be done through my head.

Would I get the drug dosages right? Drugs for kids are weight-based and a little more difficult to calculate. Would I be able to intubate the child? I'd only ever intubated adults in real-life. I had trained plenty on pediatric mannequins but had never done it on a real person. What about IV access? Little arms. Little veins. My heart was racing.

The firefighters cleared a path as I arrived. After all, I'm the paramedic right? I'm the one that's supposed to come in and use all the fancy equipment and medications and do everything to save the patient. I'm the one who is supposed to lead the call. They've been waiting for me. No pressure there.

I stepped into the nursery, looked down at the floor and saw the lifeless little body on the ground with one of the firefighters performing CPR on him. I noticed something right from the start that took me by surprise though. The infant had a tracheostomy – a hole in his throat with a connection for a ventilator in place, and sure enough, next to his bed was a ventilator.

The child, it turns out, had multiple medical problems with complications when he was first born. He was sent home after a long stay at a children's hospital, but he was essentially a vegetable. He had no quality of life and depended on a ventilator to breathe for him.

The child's father had been sleeping on the couch in the living room and woke up to the ventilator alarm going off. The circuit tubing that connects the vent to the patient had somehow disconnected and the infant was no longer receiving oxygen or artificial ventilations. The father called 911 as soon as he woke up and saw what had happened.

The fact that the baby had the tracheostomy eliminated one of the tasks that I had to worry about. I would no longer need to intubate him because our ventilation bags connect directly to the trach shiley. We picked him up and carried him to my ambulance to begin transport to the hospital. Two police officers that were on scene announced that they would lead us in – I'd never had that happen before either.

As we raced down the roadways, I verified that the breaths of air we were delivering to the child were making it to his lungs – they were. My next goal was to get IV access, but there were just no veins that I could find to use. I decided to use a device we have, called an intraosseous (IO) needle.

The IO needle is designed to penetrate the bone and deliver fluids and medications directly into the bone marrow which then delivers it to the patient's circulation, just like an IV would. These days we actually use a drill to insert the needle, but back then we didn't have that available. Instead, you would hold the device and manually screw it into the bone. So, I tried that on his right leg, but it didn't work. I then tried it on his left leg. It didn't work either.

My frustration was growing. Inserting an IO is generally an easy task, but for some reason I couldn't get it to work for me. My only remaining option was to inject the drugs directly into the trach and into his lungs where they could get absorbed and then circulated through the bloodstream. It's not the ideal option, but it is an approved option so that's what we ended up doing.

The infant's heart rhythm never changed. It was asystole the entire time. Asystole is the medical term for what most people call "flat-line." With asystole, there is no electrical activity in the heart.

31

There is nothing to shock. There is nothing more to do besides what we were already doing – CPR and administering medications. I gave a radio report to the receiving hospital so they knew that we were coming and how far out we were. I advised them we were five minutes out. It gives them time to prepare.

In my head I knew this child was dead. He was dead long before we made it to the scene. But we had to try. It's a baby. Rigor mortis had not set in, and he did not have lividity, so the "obvious" signs of prolonged death were not there. Nevertheless, I knew. We continued doing what we were doing for the remaining three or four minutes it took to get to the ER. Once we arrived, we unloaded the stretcher and rolled the patient into the resuscitation room.

I gave my report to the receiving physician and informed him that I had tried an IO in each leg but failed at getting access. He looked at me with utter disgust.

"Shame on you," he said.

At that moment I felt like the smallest person in the world. I turned around and walked out of the room. I didn't understand at first why he would say such a thing, but then it hit me. Once you stick a section of bone with an IO needle, you're not supposed to use that same area again and since I had stuck both legs (the normal places you'd put an IO), the ER staff couldn't use them. I felt terrible. What I didn't know was that one of the nurses who had known me for a long time stuck up for me after I walked out of the room. The physician was newer to the hospital and hadn't had the chance to interact with many of the medics yet.

I went out to the ambulance and my partner and I began to clean up the mess that had been made during the transport. There wasn't much to do really. It's not like it was a big, bloody trauma. We only had to use a handful of equipment and only needed to open one medication vial. My partner, John, continued to clean up while I went back inside to this little room in the corner where the EMS crews hung around to do their reports. There was paperwork that needed to be done. I could process everything later.

As I worked on the report, the ER doctor that had scolded me earlier came out, and as he approached me, he extended his hand for a handshake. I hesitated because I don't think I understood what was happening. I took his hand in mine.

"You guys did a good job," he said.

I asked him about why he was upset about the IO placement, and he confirmed with me that it was because they wouldn't be able to use those sites, but thankfully they were able to get IV access in a different location. We talked for another minute or two before he went back in to the ER.

The ER staff worked to resuscitate the infant for a good while, but in the end, it was futile and the little one year old was pronounced dead. That didn't surprise me. Like I said, I knew he was dead. We were all just going through the motions. Giving it everything we had. Hoping for a miracle, but we knew better. And just like that, my first pediatric cardiac arrest call was over. I spent a good while analyzing everything that I had done on that call. You tend to second guess yourself when it comes to calls involving kids.

In the end, I looked at the experience as both a blessing and a curse. Obviously it was a curse because a young child lost his life. But the fact that this child had no quality of life whatsoever and was now at peace is the part that I look at as a blessing. And somehow, in some small way, it made the ordeal a little easier for me to process. There are some EMS providers that can somehow go their entire careers without having a pediatric arrest. I was in the field for less than five years and had my first one. Little did I know, the second one wasn't too far behind.

*   *   *

August 2007

It hadn't even been two weeks since the call involving the infant that died, and John and I were out driving in the ambulance. It was a warm summer evening in late August, and we had spent most of the shift doing routine calls. Nothing too exciting. We were heading back to our station when we heard a call go out for a motor vehicle accident involving a pedestrian struck by a car. That was the only information that was originally dispatched. Initially, a BLS truck was dispatched on the call. I immediately picked up the radio microphone.

"Dispatch," I said, "Would you like us to respond on that call given the mechanism of injury?"

"Affirmative," the dispatcher replied.

We flipped on the lights and siren and started speeding towards the location. We were only a few minutes away from the scene.

As we got closer, we could see a police car coming from the other direction with their lights and siren on. They turned off onto the road that we would eventually go down as well. The fire department had not yet responded; the area was covered by a volunteer department so it would take some time for the guys to get to the firehouse and grab the firetrucks. A few seconds later, dispatch came onto the radio and advised that the patient was a four-year old.

You've got to be fucking kidding me.

It didn't get any better.

The police officer arrived on the scene and quickly got on the radio advising us that the child had been run over and CPR was in progress. *Here we go again*, I thought. But this time I didn't have the time to run everything through my head like I had with the infant. We were arriving on the scene. It was 8:34PM.

A large crowd had gathered in the parking lot and was standing in a circle looking down at the patient. I still remember a few people waving us over there as if we didn't have a clue where to go. I once again grabbed the pediatric jump bag and went towards the chaos.

As I walked up and saw the child I did something I had yet to do in my young career. I froze. He had clearly been run over, not just run into. Blood was pouring out of every orifice in his head. A woman was doing CPR on him and was blowing breaths through the blood and vomit spilling out of his mouth. It was his mother. A tire track could be seen going across his little chest.

He was gone. There's no coming back from this kind of injury. If it had been an adult, we wouldn't have even touched him. He would be pronounced dead right there. But it wasn't an adult. It was a child. And this child's mother was pumping on her son's chest, hoping for a miracle and at that moment she was looking to us to be her miracle.

A man nudged my shoulder and said something to the effect of, "Do something!" That brought me out of my frozen state, and my training immediately kicked in. I knelt down at the boy's head and pulled out a BVM. I cleared the airway and began to give breaths. My partner had run back to the truck to get additional equipment, so for the moment it was just me and the boy's mother.

I looked at her and said, "Just keep doing what you're doing. I'll give breaths."

It seemed to me like the right thing to do. It gave her something to keep her busy and might help prevent the feeling that she didn't do anything as her son lay motionless on the ground.

The fire department arrived on scene just a couple of minutes after we got there. I had worked with these guys for a long time and you get to know each other and what one another is capable of. A couple of them ran up, and we put a neck brace on the little boy before rolling him onto a backboard. We quickly loaded him into the ambulance and started rapid transport to the hospital.

With each chest compression, more and more blood poured out of his mouth, nose, and ears. I kept having to suction his airway to try and keep it clear. To obtain more of a definitive airway, I intubated him. We started IVs and began infusing normal saline to try and replace some of the blood volume he was losing.

The heart monitor showed a condition called Pulseless Electrical Activity, or PEA. This means that the electrical pathways are working in the heart, but there is no pulse; no blood being pumped to the body from the heart. With the tire marks present on his chest I was sure that he had sustained significant internal chest injuries. And obviously his head had been traumatized horrifically as well. For 5 minutes of eternity we worked on that boy with no change in his condition. Well, there was one change. The PEA on the cardiac monitor deteriorated to asystole. He flat-lined.

We arrived at the hospital after calling in our radio report and rushed him in to the trauma room. We moved him over to the hospital bed, and the trauma team continued doing what we had already started. They put in another IV line and continued to give fluids and medication. CPR was performed for a long time before the ER physician finally asked everyone in the room if they had any other ideas. No one did. There was just nothing else to be done. The boy was pronounced dead.

I remember standing there looking at his lifeless body and thinking *I can't do this anymore.* Two dead children in two weeks.

I'm 24 years old and this is way beyond what my brain can handle.

About that time, Brittnie, one of the nurses, came over and said, "Let's find you something to change into."

I didn't quite process what she was saying. The look of bewilderment on my face must've been obvious.

"Your shirt," she said, motioning to my uniform.

I looked down and saw what she was referring to. My shirt, from mid-chest down, was saturated with the boy's blood. And I don't mean just a little bit of blood. I mean *saturated.* As in dripping blood from my shirt onto the floor of the ER. I hadn't even noticed it. I was so involved in doing everything that I could for him that I hadn't even noticed. It had even soaked through my shirt and onto my chest.

We walked down to the OR (operating room) locker rooms where there was a cart of hospital scrubs. I took my uniform shirt off, used wet paper towels to scrub my chest clean, and put on a scrub top. I looked at my shirt for a minute. *Peroxide gets blood out of clothing.* I remember being taught that in my EMT class.

I looked at my shirt for another moment and then tossed it into the trash can. I knew right then that I did not want any reminders of that call.

A couple of hours had passed since bringing the boy to the ER. We had cleaned up the truck, restocked the equipment, taken a shower, changed clothes, and were now back at the ER to finish the report. You would look at our ambulance and wouldn't know anything like that had happened in there just a few hours earlier. And that's the point. When we're done with one call, we clean up and move on to the next call. The next patient doesn't care about what happened with the patient before them; they want your full attention and the best care that you can provide them.

I was sitting at the ER secretary's desk working on my report. John comes walking up to me.

"Do you want to deliver a baby?" he asked.

Needless to say, I was completely confused.

"What?"

"We just got a call for a pregnancy," John replied.

He handed me our truck pager which had information on it for our next run: Pregnancy-Imminent Delivery.

As we drove towards the scene, I recalled all of the other calls that I had been on that came out just like this one did. And not a single one of them resulted in me having to deliver a baby in the field. But as we got closer to the scene, something happened that made me think this one was going to be different. The fire department marked on scene and within 30 seconds they were asking for our ETA.

That can't be good.

We pulled up to the front of a trailer whose front porch was surrounded with firefighters. The only light was from the porch light and the headlights of the fire trucks and ambulance. I got out of the cab of the ambulance and opened up the side door to grab the pediatric jump bag and our OB kit. One of the firefighters walked up to me hastily.

"She feels like she has to push," he said, a bit excited.

As I walked up to the patient I asked the firefighter if anyone had done a pelvic examination yet and, not surprisingly, was told "No." When I made it to the front porch I saw the young woman, a 20 year old, sitting right on the threshold of the front door, her legs pointed outward. She was in the typical birthing position. Her mother was at her side, helping her breathe through the pain. A sheet was covering the lower portion of her body and I walked right up, didn't even introduce myself, and lifted it up so I could inspect her vagina. There were no baby parts visible, so that made me happy.

"How far apart are your contractions?" I asked.

"They're non-stop," replied her mother.

While the other guys retrieved the stretcher from the ambulance, I asked the typical assessment questions for the situation and learned that this is her fourth child, and she's 36 weeks along. Her last child was born at 35 weeks.

We weren't very far from the hospital, and the last thing that I wanted to do was deliver a baby on the front porch of a trailer in the middle of the night. We positioned the stretcher right next to her and prepared to move her to it, but before we did that I wanted to take one more look to make sure there were no baby parts starting to come out. I lifted the sheet and low and behold...there's the top of the head.

Oh, shit.

Those were the words that I'm sure went through my head. As a matter of fact, I'm told those were the words that came out of my mouth. I don't necessarily believe that though. I immediately grabbed our OB kit. The thing about our OB kits is that they're sealed up like a bag of chips. Have you ever been opening a bag of chips for the first time and you're having trouble getting it to open? You pull harder and then POP goes the bag and chips fly everywhere, right? Well, just imagine the same thing happening with me and that OB kit. The contents of the bag scattered and while the firefighters worked to gather it up for me, I quickly made as sterile a field as I could around the mother's vagina, put my hand on top of the baby's head to prevent an explosive delivery and told her to push.

It only took another two or three pushes and out came the little head. I used the bulb syringe to suction the baby's mouth and nose, made sure the umbilical cord was not wrapped around its neck and then got ready for the next round of pushing.

With this being her fourth child, the mom needed very little coaching. After just a few more pushes, out came the baby. The whole time this was happening all I could think about was something that I was told my very first night of EMT school years earlier: if you drop the baby, pick it up. Well thankfully, I did <u>not</u> drop the baby.

I dried it and stimulated it and began smiling from ear to ear when the crying started. Once the baby was dried, I wrapped it up and held it up so the mother could see.

"You've got yourself a baby girl."

A second ambulance arrived on scene to take care of the mother. Since the baby was premature, I had decided to call for a second paramedic unit as a precaution. We loaded the mother and baby into my ambulance and the second paramedic rode with me so I'd have a second set of hands.

On the way to the hospital, we kept the little one dry and warm, gave her a little bit of oxygen, checked her glucose, and kept a close eye on her. I called in the radio report to the hospital and once we arrived at the ER we were directed to go into the very same room that we had brought the 4 year old in to earlier that evening.

The ER doctor took a quick look at her before the NICU team came down with an isolette, put her in it and carted her away for observation. The ER staff couldn't believe it. Imagine the luck that one crew would have to go from doing CPR on a 4 year old to delivering a baby. It was absolutely unbelievable. I can't imagine that that's the only time something like that has happened, but I also can't imagine that it's something that happens often.

I stayed in the ER to finish up my report for the run. It actually required two separate reports; one for the mother and one for the baby. Once I was done, my partner and I walked down to the NICU to check on the baby girl that we had just delivered.

She was lying in a baby warmer, perfectly pink in color and super active, moving her little legs and arms about. The monitor showed that her vital signs were normal. I put my finger to her hand and out of reflex she grabbed it. I couldn't stop smiling.

This night of tragedy had taken such an unanticipated, but very welcome, turn. As I looked into her eyes all I could think was the complete opposite of the thoughts that went through my head earlier in the evening.

There's nothing else in this world that I'd rather do.

41

4

Expect the Unexpected

If there's one thing that I've learned after nearly 20 years in this profession it's that no two days are alike. That's actually one of the things that keeps me coming back to work day after day; the not-knowing. Granted, you're going to have your frequent flyers and your typical chest pain and breathing difficulty calls, but from time to time you are sent on calls that leave you scratching your head, wondering what happened, how it happened, and what you're supposed to do about it.

*   *   *

December 2009

It was not a particularly busy day, given that it was New Year's Eve. Although I'd come to learn that a shift in EMS on NYE was either slow as a snail or balls-to-the-wall, this shift was somewhere in the middle. We had just finished up with dropping off a patient at the ER; nothing special, just a routine call. We reloaded our stretcher and equipment into the ambulance and had climbed back into the cab when the familiar sound of our tones emitted from the radio.

"Medic 30, respond to the corner of 8th Avenue and 19th street on a gunshot wound," the dispatcher said. "You'll be responding for City Fire."

We typically covered the area of our county that was outside the city limits while the city fire department covered everything within the city limits. Obviously all of their ambulances must've been tied up on runs since we were being sent on a call within their response area. As a matter of fact it was literally just twelve blocks down the road from where we were.

As we made our way down the street we could see the fire engine and police cars arriving at the intersection. Personnel exiting their apparatus moved to the suspected patient who was laying on the sidewalk just off of the road. As we pulled up alongside them, we could see that the fire personnel had already placed a bandage on his head and were actively bandaging his hand. I exited the vehicle and moved towards them.

"What do y'all have?" I inquired as I moved closer. One of the police officers stepped over to me.

"He told me that he was just walking along, minding his own business when someone pulled up, jumped out of their car and started swinging a machete at him."

"A machete?" I asked, slightly taken aback.

"Yeah. Dispatch put it out as a GSW, but he's not shot," the officer continued.

"What kinds of injuries does he have fellas?" I asked the men off of the engine company.

"He's got a scalping on the left side and near-amputations of two fingers on the right hand," the company captain reported. "He's getting awfully lethargic, too."

The patient was a black male, and although there was not a lot of external blood loss he was looking quite pale. I leaned over him to do a quick assessment.

He was conscious but very lethargic. His airway was clear. The bleeding to his head wound had been controlled by the fire department's pressure dressing. He didn't have any obvious injuries to his thorax, arms, or legs. The near-amputations to his fingers were probably the result of him putting his hand up as a defensive move. The probable loss of his fingers may have in fact saved his life.

Fire personnel advised that the patient's skull appeared intact and non-fractured; the wound to his head seemed to only be an avulsion. But his altered level of consciousness was concerning to me.

Why is this guy so lethargic?

He hasn't lost much blood. He doesn't appear to have sustained any significant injuries, so why is he so altered? It's possible that the blow to his head may have caused a closed head injury, but I don't think it's likely. Regardless, I knew we needed to err on the side of caution and go ahead and take over his airway just to be safe.

We loaded him onto the stretcher and got him into the ambulance and out of the elements. Once in the ambulance, my partner Amanda assessed his vital signs. Amanda was an awesome EMT. I didn't work with her on a regular basis because she was part-time, but she loved medicine (she actually loved medicine so much that she went to medical school and became a doctor).

"Vitals are OK," she said. "But his respirations are starting to get a little shallow."

"Go ahead and throw in an IV," I delegated as I started to take out my airway kit.

"What's your plan?" Bill, the captain, asked. "You going to tube him?"

"Yep."

The patient's bleeding had been controlled by this point and taking over his airway would be a simple task. I still wasn't entirely sure what was causing his altered level of consciousness, but I'd rather be ahead of the eight ball than behind it.

My partner had successfully placed two IVs in either arm. I grabbed two syringes, drew up the appropriate doses of the necessary medications to place the patient into an induced coma, administered the medications, and waited. The medications generally kick in rather quickly, but it's during those few seconds that you get a little nervous.

In a matter of seconds these medications are going to paralyze this patient. Every muscle, including the ones he uses to breathe will cease to work. At that moment I will have precious few seconds to use my training and equipment to visualize his airway anatomy and slip a breathing tube into his trachea. I had done it several times throughout my career, but I was still a young medic and this procedure still made me nervous. And I didn't view that nervousness as a bad thing.

It was easy to notice when the medications kicked in: the patient stopped breathing. The next step was to place the laryngoscope into his mouth, displace the tongue, pull the jaw open, and visualize the vocal cords. It was not a difficult task with this patient. I had a clear view of his vocal cords and maintained visual contact of them as I passed the endotracheal tube through and into the trachea. Once the tube was in I removed the laryngoscope, inflated the tube's balloon which creates a seal around the tube, and placed the bag-valve-mask on the tube.

Squeezing the BVM a few times, I listened over his chest for the presence of air movement through his lungs. Perfect. I then listened for air movement over the stomach. None. Perfect. The tube was in the correct position. I secured it in place and then motioned to the driver that we were good to go.

The trip to the hospital was quick, after all it was just down the street. I called in a quick report on the radio so they knew we were coming. A minute or two later, we were pulling into the ambulance bay. We got our equipment in order, unloaded the stretcher from the ambulance, and moved inside.

Once inside the ER we were directed to take the patient to Trauma 1, where we found the trauma team waiting on us. Being a smaller community hospital, they stabilized the patient before arranging transfer by helicopter to the regional trauma center.

The patient's head CT ended up being negative; no brain injury. No one really knows why he had the sudden change in his level of consciousness. Most likely it was just a bad concussion. His scalp injury was repaired and he ended up losing two of his fingers, but it could've been much worse.

At least he got to live to tell the tale of his drive-by machete-hacking.

*　　　*　　　*

June 2011

It hadn't been a particularly busy day. Ashlee was my partner for the shift, and we had just finished eating dinner and were heading back to our station when we decided to stop by Central Dispatch to visit Amanda, a colleague of ours and a dispatcher for the county.

The county dispatch center was located in the basement of the county's security center, which also housed the sheriff's office and jail. When we arrived, we parked in the employee parking lot and had to wait at a secure entrance for Amanda to come up and let us in. Once inside the building we made our way down to the basement, going through two additional security doors which required badge access to open.

Once in the dispatch center we found that things were relatively quiet.

"What are you guys out doing?" Amanda asked.

"Not much, hopefully," Ashlee said in jest.

"Just got done eating, heading back to station," I said. "You guys been busy in here?"

"Not really. I came on at six and we've been pretty quiet since," Amanda said.

She and Ashlee continued conversing for a moment while I snuck a peek at the Computer Aided Dispatch (CAD) screen to see what types of calls were going on in the county. There wasn't much to see. Amanda wasn't kidding. It had been a slow night. But the thing you learn about public safety is that a slow night can change in the blink of an eye.

"Did you say he's still in the windshield?"

I heard the words come from another dispatcher sitting a few feet away. My ears perked up, and I walked over to see what was going on.

"Is he conscious?" the dispatcher asked the caller.

I looked over his shoulder at his screen as he continued to type in information that the caller was giving him. So far, the information consisted of:

47

Car vs. moped. Male subject through windshield. Breathing. Unconscious.

I made note of the incident location and realized that it was our response district.

"Ashlee, we've got to go."

"What is it?"

"Car versus moped with a guy stuck in the windshield."

"What?!"

We said a quick goodbye to Amanda and made our way out the door, down the hallway, and up the first flight of stairs. And then we were stopped cold in our tracks. The door was locked, and we did not have Amanda with us to use her card to get us out.

"Shit!" I exclaimed before turning around to run back down the stairs. I made my way back down the hallway to the dispatch room and knocked on the door. The door unlocked and as I opened it, Amanda looked over at me.

"What's the matter?" she asked.

"Can't get out."

She got up and started walking towards me. I'm pretty sure I saw her roll her eyes in the process.

"All you have to do is hit the little button next to the door and they will let you out, but here, I'll just go with you," she said.

She led us out of the building, we jumped into the ambulance and started towards the scene of the collision. A BLS ambulance was also sent to the scene due to a report of multiple patients.

While we were en route, my morbid curiosity was getting the best of me. I was kind of hoping we would make it to the scene before the fire department removed the guy from the windshield. I was interested to see exactly what that looked like. I would soon find out.

As we approached the scene, numerous emergency vehicles were already present. Officers were directing traffic around the vehicles involved while fire department personnel were tending to the patients. The other ambulance had arrived just prior to us. I put the truck in park and made my way to the car and saw exactly what I was picturing.

A male adult, who had been riding as a passenger on a moped, was ejected from the moped when it was struck from behind. He went through the windshield of the car that struck him and landed in the passenger seat. His legs were still up and over the dashboard onto the hood of the car. He had multiple lacerations on his head and arms. He was breathing but unconscious.

One of the firefighters was inside the car, assessing the patient as I walked up.

"What's his status?"

"He's breathing, but he's completely out."

"Alright, let's get him out of here," I said.

The firefighter proceeded to put a c-collar on the patient and then with the help of additional firefighters, we pulled the man from the car and got him onto a backboard before moving him to the stretcher.

"Does anyone know if they've got a bird coming?" I asked.

"Yeah," the firefighter replied. "I think they auto-launched them."

It was not uncommon for Central Dispatch to auto-launch medical helicopters to scenes where the mechanism of injury was significant. Patients suffering major traumatic injuries often fared better when transported by air directly from the scene to a regional trauma center.

Once the patient was on the stretcher, an oxygen mask was placed on him. Other than a slight moan or groan, he was still unconscious. We made our way to the ambulance as one of the EMTs from the other ambulance approached me.

"Do you guys need any help?" Kim asked.

"If you guys don't have a patient, sure." I said.

"The driver of the moped is okay. She wants to be transported just to get checked out, but she seems fine. My partner's with her."

"Sounds good to me. We could use a hand. Probably going to tube this guy," I replied.

Once we had the patient loaded into the ambulance, I placed an IV and began to prep for the RSI procedure; there was no question that this patient needed to be intubated. He was about 6'2" and weighed roughly 230 pounds. His head was shaved and he had several tattoos. Not to be stereotypical or anything, but the thought went through my head that he had done some time in prison. Nonetheless, after estimating his weight, I drew up the appropriate medications in preparation for the procedure.

We spent a few minutes pre-oxygenating him, and then it was show time. I could hear the sound of the approaching helicopter overhead. They would be landing in a church's parking lot just down the street from where my ambulance was sitting. My goal was to get this guy intubated before they made it to the ambulance so that way we could just get him packaged and on his way to the trauma center.

"Okay, let's do this," I said before pushing the first medication, the sedative etomidate. Shortly after, I quickly pushed the paralyzing drug, succinylcholine. I waited the obligatory 30-45 seconds and then opened the patient's mouth, inserting the laryngoscope on the right side, sweeping the tongue to the left. But then, something happened I was not expecting.

He gagged.

It shouldn't have happened. Not only had he been deeply unconscious, but I had also given him a potent sedative *and* a paralyzing drug; he shouldn't be able to *do* anything. But he gagged, and I mean *gagged*. The next thing I knew he suddenly began thrashing his head side to side and started to try and sit up off of the stretcher.

"Whoa, whoa, whoa! Hold him down!" I exclaimed.

Ashlee and one of the firefighters tried pushing down on him to get his head back down, but he was fighting. With his head injury, he had slipped into a primitive survival mode. He didn't know what he was doing. Combine that with his size and strength, and we were in a bad place. The next thing I heard was: "Chris!" It was Kim calling out my name, but there was something off about her voice; it was like it was muffled or something. I looked to my left and discovered why.

The patient had his hand wrapped tightly around Kim's throat. He was choking her. She was attempting to pry his hand off but was not having success doing so. I reached over and also attempted to peel his fingers off of her. Meanwhile, the others continued to try and push

51

him down, fighting his fit of rage. I reached over and put the palm of my hand against his forehead and stood over him, pushing all of my weight into him. His grip released from Kim's throat. She gasped for air and sat back onto the bench seat.

Ashlee and one of the firefighters worked to get the patient's hands secured to the stretcher. The back doors of the ambulance opened to reveal the flight crew had arrived.

"Hey, guys," the flight nurse said. "How's it going in here?"

I looked at her and made a facial expression that I'm sure spoke volumes. I went on to explain what had happened. We checked the IV to make sure it had not blown. That would've explained why the medications did not appear to work on him. But the IV was fine. We couldn't figure out what happened. The drug choices were correct. The doses were correct. Regardless, we still had to get him under control.

The flight crew quickly drew up medications of their own and administered them through the IV line. The patient subsequently fell unconscious again, successfully sedated this time. The flight nurse, Michelle, moved into position and intubated the man with no further difficulty.

"So, I guess this is you paying me back, huh," I said. Michelle was the flight nurse that responded on a bad motorcycle accident I had been on a few months prior. Neither she nor her partner could get that patient intubated, but I was able to. "I owe you one," I recall her saying on that run. Well, I guess this was it.

We confirmed that the tube was placed correctly and secured it. We then got the patient packaged and prepped for transport. As the flight crew and some of the firefighters moved the patient to the helicopter, I turned my attention to Kim.

52

"You okay?" I asked.

"Yeah, I think so," Kim said, rubbing her reddened neck.

"Sorry. I'm not sure what the hell happened," I said. "Obviously the line was good. Their meds worked. So, I don't know."

"It's okay. It's not a big deal," she said before returning to her ambulance in order to transport the other patient to the hospital.

But it was a big deal. As I started to clean up my ambulance, I thought about the fact that a lot of people forget that EMS providers face dangerous situations every day, just like their counterparts in law enforcement and the fire service. Sure, we may not get into shootouts or run into fires, but we face violence, exposure to disease, vehicle accidents, and the risk of being hit while working a car accident. It's more than just taking someone to the hospital. It can truly be a dangerous job.

*　　*　　*

May 2019

It was a warm but overcast day in early May. Scattered rain showers had been coming and going for most of the morning but had seemed to quit for the most part. My partner, Heavin, and I were taking advantage of the break in the rain to wash the ambulance. Lindsay, an EMT student from a class I was teaching, was riding with us for the shift. Like most students, Lindsay was hoping to get something worthwhile during her ride time. What she didn't know was she was about to witness something that in 17 years of practice I had never seen happen.

Just as we finished rinsing the truck off, the tones sounded on the overhead speakers in the firehouse. We were dispatched to one of the county parks on a report of a male adult actively seizing. We pulled the hose back into the bay, closed the overhead door, climbed into the ambulance, and marked en route to the scene.

We hadn't been en route but for a couple of minutes when the dispatcher came across the radio with an update.

"Be advised this call is being upgraded to a cardiac arrest. CPR is in progress at this time."

I looked over at Heavin, "Well that escalated quickly."

Meanwhile, a sheriff's deputy who had been on patrol not far from the park was arriving on scene. As he pulled into the park, he was directed to a crowd of people who had gathered about 150' from the finish line of a triathlon that was taking place. He pulled his vehicle off the side of the drive and quickly exited, walking to the rear and opening the rear hatch. From inside the rear compartment he grabbed his AED and walked towards the group of bystanders performing CPR on the unresponsive man.

The deputy knelt down and opened the AED, removing the defibrillation pads. He placed them on the man's chest and the AED began to analyze his heart's rhythm.

"Stand clear," the AED's computer voice advised. "Analyzing now. Do not touch the patient."

After about 5 seconds of analysis, the AED once again spoke.

"Shock advised."

The AED charged up and when ready sounded an alarm indicating the shock was ready to be delivered.

"Everybody clear," the deputy commanded.

After ensuring that no one was touching the patient the deputy pressed the "shock" button sending a current of electricity through the patient's heart. Once the shock had been delivered, the deputy continued performing chest compressions.

"Can I get an ETA on the ambulance?" the deputy asked his dispatcher via his radio.

The request for the ETA was relayed to us when we were less than two minutes from the scene.

"We're less than two out," I advised the dispatcher over the radio. "Can the deputy advise a better location of the patient?"

Prior to that moment, the only information we had been given was that the patient was in the park; otherwise, no specific information had been relayed to us.

"He advises they're just inside the main entrance of the park," the dispatcher relayed. "Once you enter the park, turn right and you should see them. He's also advising the patient is improving."

Heavin and I looked at each other wondering to what extent the patient was improving or if he even was.

We pulled into the park's entrance and around the corner to find the deputy and the crowd of bystanders kneeling next to the patient. However, no one was doing CPR. As we pulled up, I looked closer and could see that the patient's color was normal and his eyes were open. We exited the ambulance, grabbed our equipment, and made our way over to them.

"What do you have?" I asked the deputy.

He brought me up to speed on the events that had transpired prior to our arrival. Following the delivery of the shock, he did another minute of CPR. The patient began making sounds and started breathing on his own. Just prior to our arrival, he opened his eyes.

I knelt down next to the patient and assessed him in my head.

Airway is open. Breathing is normal. Skin is normal in color.

"Can you tell me your name, sir?"

"Mark," the patient groggily answered. "What happened?"

"We're trying to figure that out," I replied. "But it looks like your heart may have gone into an irregular rhythm."

"What do you mean?" he asked.

"Are you having any chest pain or difficulty breathing?"

Instead of answering, Mark began to get up off of the ground. I put my hands on his shoulders, trying to keep him from getting up.

"No, no. Let's stay still for a minute," I requested.

"No, I need to get up," Mark demanded. And he started to stand up.

We helped him onto his feet and brought the stretcher to his side. Mark brushed off some loose gravel that was stuck to his legs and arms. I made note of small abrasions on his extremities.

"You OK?" I asked, concerned about him being on his feet, afraid that he might re-arrest at any moment.

"I'm fine."

"Let's get you in the ambulance and take a look at you."

He sat down on the stretcher and we secured him in place. We raised the stretcher up and rolled him towards the back of the ambulance.

"Is that the finish line?" Mark asked, noticing that we were only about fifty yards from the finish line.

"Yeah, that's it," Heavin confirmed.

We loaded the stretcher into the back of the ambulance, climbed in, and started our work-up of Mark. While Heavin began to put the cardiac leads on his chest to obtain a 12-lead ECG, I placed the blood pressure cuff on his arm and pulse oximeter probe on his finger. We ran the 12-lead and I looked over it once it printed out.

I was surprised by what I saw. Mark saw my expression.

"What's wrong?" he asked.

I looked up from the ECG.

"Surprisingly, nothing. The ECG looks OK," I said.

I grabbed a tourniquet to put on Mark's arm in order to start an IV.

"Ok, Mark, first thing we're going to do is throw an IV in and draw some blood."

"I don't want to go to the hospital," he said.

I stopped cold in my tracks and looked up at him, shocked.

"Oh, you're going to the hospital."

"No, I don't want to go. You said everything looked alright."

"Mark, your heart stopped. Bystanders had to do CPR on you and shock you with a defibrillator to get it started again. I know your ECG looks okay right now, but that doesn't mean that there's not a very serious problem. You *need* to go," I pleaded.

"No, thank you."

"Okay, well hang on just a minute," I said before getting up and stepping out the side of the ambulance.

I looked around to see if I could find Mark's wife but couldn't locate her anywhere. Brent, one of the deputies, was nearby.

"Hey, Brent," I motioned at him to come over.

"Where's his wife?"

"She already started for the hospital," he replied.

"Well, he's refusing to go."

"You're shitting me," Brent said.

Dayton, the deputy who had performed CPR on Mark, overheard my conversation with Brent and walked to the back of the ambulance, opening the door.

"Mark, buddy, what's going on?" Dayton asked.

"I really don't need to go. I'm fine," Mark said. "You can't make me go."

He looked past Dayton towards the finish line.

"Is that the finish line?" Mark asked.

"That's it," I replied.

After several more minutes of negotiating, we were finally able to reach a compromise with Mark: if we would let him cross the finish line then he agreed he'd go to the hospital for evaluation. I suggested we could push him over it on the stretcher, but he was having none of that. Ultimately, he agreed to let us walk alongside him with our heart monitor still attached to him. And that's exactly what we did.

As we crossed the finish line, Mark received a round of applause from everyone in attendance. During the short walk from the ambulance across the line, his heart rhythm remained unchanged. Although it was not what I preferred, if it was what got him to agree to go to the ER then I was up for it.

By this point, Mark's wife Jennifer had returned to the scene. One of the deputies was able to make contact with her and informed her of the new development in the situation. And she was not happy.

"What are you doing?!" she exclaimed as she walked up to Mark.

"I'm fine," he said.

"No, you are not fine, Mark. I was literally doing CPR on you not even 15 minutes ago."

Mark was in denial. I could tell. The expression on his face spoke volumes. He simply did not believe anything anyone was saying to him. And my realization of his denial made what came next unsurprising.

"I'm not going," Mark said.

"What? You promised me you'd go if we let you walk over the finish line," Dayton argued.

"Look, I get you guys are concerned, but I'm okay," Mark insisted.

I stepped over to the side to speak to the deputies out of earshot of Mark.

"I don't know what to do here. I can't force him to go," I said.

"We'll just ID him," Brent suggested.

An ID, or immediate detention, is an option provided to law enforcement officers to compel someone to seek medical attention when they are not within their right mind or are a danger to themselves or others.

"On what grounds?" I asked.

"He's confused," Brent replied.

"But he's not. He's in denial, but he's not confused," I said.

At that point, I stepped back over to Mark and asked him a series of questions to confirm that he was within a normal state of mind. He answered every single question correctly. The deputies were in agreement there was nothing that could be done from a legal standpoint.

We then conferred with Mark's wife and went back and forth with him for a few more minutes before finally reaching a resolution. Mark's wife would drive him to the hospital and we would follow in the ambulance in the event something would happen.

Mark reluctantly agreed to this. He got into the passenger seat of the family car and Jennifer, obviously upset, hopped into the driver's seat. The deputies also provided an escort. On the way to the hospital, I called and spoke to the charge nurse, Hannah, and told her to expect the patient, explaining what had happened. The drive to the ER took about 10 minutes but luckily was uneventful.

When we arrived at the hospital, we helped Mark inside and turned him over to the ER nurses. Apparently, he was not the nicest of patients with the hospital staff, arguing that he didn't really think the situation was as bad as we had made it out to be. He was treated in the ER where his ECG and lab work came back normal, but when he was taken to the cardiac cath lab, his left anterior descending artery was found to be 90% blocked. Blockage of that artery can lead to the fatal heart attack commonly known as "The Widowmaker."

I guess it was a good idea that we kept pushing him to go. They opened up the vessel, and he was able to go home the next day. Mark's story proves that quick CPR by bystanders and early defibrillation can make the difference between life and death. Mark may have been in denial about the events of that day, but there's no denying that someone was watching over him.

- 5 -

Between a Rock and a Hard Place

It doesn't take very long in this business, if you want to call it a business, to figure out that people tend to get themselves stuck in some fairly odd places. Sometimes, the fact that they are stuck is the sole problem that they are having, while other times they may be experiencing an additional medical emergency. In those situations you quickly find that you're left having to deal with more than one issue in a less-than-favorable environment.

*   *   *

May 2007

It was a warm Tuesday morning in mid-May, and my partner John and I were returning to our station after dropping a patient off at the hospital when the dispatcher came across the radio, changing our plans.

"Medic 30, respond on a male subject, altered mental status."

We wrote down the address, turned the truck around, flipped on the lights and siren, and started towards the residence. We arrived to the patient's residence in less than eight minutes to find the local volunteer fire department already on scene. As we exited the truck, one of the firefighters approached me.

"He's stuck in the tub," he said.

"He's what?" I asked.

"He's stuck in the bathtub. And he's not little."

We grabbed our gear and made our way into the house, down a short hallway, and into the bathroom where we found other members from the fire department standing beside a small, blue bathtub. Sitting inside the tub was the patient: a naked, wet, and roughly 400lb man.

"Every time we try to touch him, he swings at us," said one of the firefighters on scene.

"What do we know about his history?" I asked.

"Diabetic. COPD. High blood pressure."

I turned to speak to the patient's wife in an attempt to get an understanding of what had happened. She informed me that the patient had advised her he was not feeling well and was going to take a shower. A short while after he had been in there the wife went to check on him and found him sitting on the floor of the tub, wedged in, and mildly combative with confusion.

My initial thought process was simple: he's a diabetic, his blood sugar is most likely low. But the patient was also presenting with signs of respiratory issues. I could hear audible wheezing and his work of breathing was increased, but because of his state of confusion, every attempt to provide oxygen to him was met with resistance.

I happened to notice a vein running along his calf that looked suitable for an IV. If I could access it successfully we'd be able to check his blood sugar level and give him medication to bring it up if it was indeed low. Plus, the fact that his legs were so large made it nearly impossible for him to move them, so he wasn't going to be able to put up much of a fight.

I gathered up my equipment, prepped the area with an alcohol prep and proceeded to insert an IV. He wasn't happy about it, but there wasn't really much he could do to stop me. His large abdomen kept him from being able to lean forward and hit me like he was trying to do, and my suspicion that he wouldn't be able to move his legs much was confirmed. The IV was placed and we were able to use some of the blood from the insertion to test his blood glucose level.

It was low. *Not surprising.*

I hooked up an IV of saline and prepared to administer some dextrose to him. Once I was sure that the saline was running in without issue, I proceeded to push the syringe of dextrose. IV dextrose will usually lead to an improvement in the patient's condition within two minutes of administration.

So we waited.

And waited.

And waited.

But there was no change. He was still confused. He didn't recognize us, his wife, or the situation. I rechecked his sugar. It was now within normal limits, but his presentation was the same. There was obviously something else going on. I considered the possibility that perhaps his altered mental status was due to a decreased oxygen level, but his pulse oximetry reading wasn't really that bad.

Despite his resistance to our help he did let us place an oxygen mask with a breathing treatment on his face, and he actually left it there, so that was something. The next priority was going to be getting him out of the tub. The first technique we attempted made the most sense to us: simply grab him by the hand and try pulling him up. Maybe he'll recognize the fact that we're trying to help him and will assist us.

Nope. Bad idea. Instead of trying to help us he actually took a swing at us. Plan A was not going to work.

The patient was simply too large to simply manhandle out of the tub, so we were going to have to come up with some way to lift him out. The fact that he was large, wet, and naked provided less-than-ideal circumstances to work with.

"Why don't we just cut a big hole in the wall and pull him out the side of the house," an overzealous firefighter suggested.

"We're not there yet," I said.

The fact that the patient was not in a dire condition allowed us some time to figure out the safest way to get him out. After a few minutes of brainstorming, we finally concocted a plan. We would use several bed sheets wrapped around his body and under his arms to lift him up and then slide him across the edge of the tub and onto a chair which sat level with the tub.

I walked out of the bathroom to go to the truck to get some bed sheets. When I made it into the living room, I found my partner sitting on the stretcher with his feet propped up.

"What are you doing?"

"What? Not like there was room in there for me too," he said.

I rolled my eyes and laughed. Technically, he wasn't wrong.

I went to the ambulance, grabbed some sheets, and made my way back to the bathroom. We made "snakes" out of the sheets, twisting them around themselves, and then wrapped them around the patient's chest, essentially making a makeshift harness. One of the guys from the fire department grabbed on to one sheet while I grabbed the other. I looked over at him.

"Ready?" I asked.

He nodded his head and we began to pull up on the sheet harness. The patient immediately began to fight against us, grabbing the sheets himself and pulling us downward towards the tub.

"Grab his arms!" I shouted.

One of the firefighters leaned in around me and pushed his arms down off of the sheets while we continued to pull. The patient continued to yell and attempt to thwart our efforts. We continued to pull against his resisting weight.

"Pull! Pull! Pull!"

A spotter was watching to see how close the patient's bottom was to the lip of the tub. We continued to pull the patient up as the other fireman proceeded to hold his arms down.

"His ass is over the lip!" the spotter shouted.

"Chair!"

The spotter reached over and grabbed the chair that we had moved into the bathroom and placed it against the side of the tub. We pulled the patient over the lip and slid him onto the chair. We positioned him in such a way that he was sitting on the chair with his feet still inside the tub. But the bulk of him was finally out.

Once he was on the chair, he calmed down. We gave him a few minutes to come to his senses before pulling his feet the rest of the way over the side of the tub.

"You okay?" I asked him.

He didn't speak, but he did nod his head in affirmation. We moved the stretcher into position and helped him stand to get onto it. He didn't need much in the way of treatment during transport. He looked exhausted though. Hell, I was exhausted.

Once at the ER, we transferred him to a hospital bed and I gave a report to the receiving nurse.

"So, you said he was *stuck* in the bathtub when you got there?" she asked.

"Uh, huh."

"How'd you get him out?"

I looked at her and could only come up with one thing to say: "Well, it sure as hell wasn't graceful."

*   *   *

February 2012

Every so often EMS is dispatched to a funeral home. Typically, the reasons range from people falling or, more commonly, passing out from the stress they're often experiencing while attending the funeral of a loved one. Personally, I've been dispatched to a funeral home two or three times, but it wasn't until February 2012 that I had my first dispatch to an actual cemetery.

"Engine 41, Rescue 41, TAC 41, Medic 30 respond on a report of a male subject trapped in an open gravesite."

The dispatch came over the radio right as I took my first bite of food. I was working with Ashlee for the shift, and we had just sat down to eat lunch. It's pretty much Murphy's Law of EMS that if you try to eat or sleep, you will get a call. And Murphy came through.

"Did she just say what I think she said?"

Ashlee nodded her head, also with an obvious perplexed look on her face.

"Well, that's different," I said while gathering my food and throwing it into a brown paper bag to take with us.

It took us about eight minutes to get to the scene. The local fire department had already arrived and was sizing up the situation as we pulled the ambulance down the gravel road which ran through the cemetery. As we exited the ambulance, I was looking towards where everyone had gathered but could not quite figure out what was going on. We grabbed our gear and approached the scene which is when the gravity of the situation became clear.

A crew had been in the process of lowering a 3000lb burial vault into the gravesite when the support beams running across the top of the site collapsed. A worker who had been standing on one of the beams fell during the collapse and now his leg was pinned between the vault and the support beam. He was conscious and breathing, so that was a plus.

Matt, one of the fire department captains, was down in the hole examining the area beneath the vault to determine the best way to stabilize it. Other members of the department were moving quickly to bring appropriate cribbing and other supportive equipment to the gravesite.

Ashlee and I watched from above as I ran different injury scenarios through my head. The vault was sitting directly on the man's femur, which could cause massive bleeding if fractured. His pants did not appear torn nor were they blood-stained, so I was assuming that there was no open fracture present.

"Hey, can I get down there and take a look at him?" I asked Matt.

"Should be okay," he said.

Should be?

I climbed down into the hole and stood at the patient's side.

"Hey, I'm Chris, I'm a paramedic."

"Brett."

"How you doing, Brett?"

"Been better."

"I can imagine. How's your pain?"

"Leg's mostly numb, but what I can feel hurts like hell."

"I'm going to help you with that. Are you allergic to any meds?"

He shook his head.

"Okay. Well, here's the plan. I'm going to put an IV in your arm and give you some pain medication, try and take the edge off a little bit."

"Sounds good to me," Brett said through clenched teeth.

Ashlee passed our jump bag down to me, and I removed the necessary equipment to establish the IV line. After checking his vital signs, I prepped his left arm and placed the IV before drawing up the medication and administering it. Because of Brett's precarious position, I needed to be very careful about how much medication I was giving him. He was obviously in a lot of pain, so I wanted to give him enough to relieve some of that pain, but I needed to make sure I didn't give him too much and drop his blood pressure or impair his breathing. I gave the medication a minute or so to circulate.

"Are you feeling it, yet?"

"Yeah, a little," Brett said. "Just get me out of here!"

"We're working on it, bud," Matt said.

Chuck, the Incident Commander, stepped over to the side of the gravesite.

"Hey, Chris. Air-Evac is saying they're five minutes out. They're going to land in the high school's parking lot," Chuck conveyed.

Until then, I hadn't even been told that a helicopter had been requested nor was I sure that one was needed. Brett had escaped worse injury by a stroke of luck. When the support beams fell, the vault leaned away from Brett instead of towards him which ultimately saved him from being squashed. It appeared that his only injury was the isolated leg injury. But there were a few complications that I was worried about.

If the vault falling onto his leg had damaged any of his blood vessels, it was possible that the pressure from it was keeping those damaged vessels from bleeding. Once the vault was lifted from his leg, the vessels would be able to bleed freely, potentially causing catastrophic blood loss. Alternatively, if circulation to his leg had been compromised by the pressure of the vault, there was the possibility that toxins were accumulating in his lower leg, and if that was the case, once the pressure was released those toxins could flood his cardiovascular system and cause major problems. The sooner we freed him, the less likely that scenario was.

Workers from the cemetery's crew had made the suggestion to the fire department that they use their lift to raise the vault off of Brett, especially considering the vault was already chained to it. The firefighters didn't necessarily like that idea because they were concerned about the vault shifting and causing more injury to Brett. Instead, they continued using cribbing and struts to stabilize the vault, with the intention to use pneumatic air bags to lift the vault from Brett's leg.

Meanwhile, I was working on a plan to get Brett out of the hole once he was free. We didn't have room to place him on a backboard or use a stokes basket to get him out. I decided to secure him to an extrication vest instead. The extrication vest was seldom used in EMS and was designed for removal of patients with possible neck or spine injuries from a vehicle involved in an accident. Although there was no reason to believe that Brett had sustained a neck or back injury, the vest would provide us a means to package him and give us something to grab onto (the vest has handles on it) to lift him up and out of the hole.

After further coordination with the cemetery's crew, the fire department had decided to take an approach that combined the plans of using the ground's crew's equipment and the air bags to free Brett. The machine would be used to hold tension on the vault with the chain while the air bags would be inflated just enough to free Brett's pinned leg. Once everyone was briefed on the plan and all of the equipment was ready, we prepared to put the plan into action.

It didn't take much inflation of the air bags before the vault shifted, but luckily it moved in the opposite direction, and as its weight shifted it freed Brett's leg. It wasn't quite what the plan was, but it worked. I manually stabilized Brett's leg as two firefighters from above grabbed the handles on the extrication vest and pulled Brett up over the side of the grave. We then moved him to the nearby stretcher. I climbed out of the grave, removed my trauma shears, and cut his pant leg so I could take a closer look at his leg. I was shocked by what I saw.

There was no obvious injury. The area was reddened, but otherwise there was nothing that stuck out. No obvious fracture. No deformity. No bleeding. Nothing. Brett was already getting feeling back in his leg. Because I simply could not believe that his leg was able to escape that type of accident unscathed, I went ahead and splinted it, out of an abundance of caution. At this point, I decided to cancel the helicopter and send them home.

En route to the hospital, I gave him a little more pain medication and monitored his vital signs, which remained perfectly stable. When we arrived at the ER, we rolled the stretcher into Trauma Room 3 and moved Brett to the hospital bed while giving the trauma team a report of what had transpired.

"Good luck, Brett," I said as I made my way out of the trauma room.

"Thank you," he said.

About fifteen minutes later while I was finishing up some paperwork, Ashlee walked up to me to inform me that Brett's wife was there and wanted to see me.

"Why?" I asked.

"I don't know. I think she just wants to thank you."

"Oh, okay."

I made my way down the hallway and back into Trauma 3. Brett's wife was standing at his side, holding his hand tightly in hers.

"Are you the one that got him out?" she asked.

"Well, I'm one of them, yes ma'am," I said.

Before I could get the sentence out, she had walked over to me and wrapped her arms around me, giving me one of the strongest hugs I'd been given in a long time.

"Thank you so much," she said through sniffles and tears of joy and relief.

"It's okay. It's no problem. It's our job. And I think he's going to be just fine."

"The doctor says he doesn't think it's broken but wants to get an x-ray to be sure," the wife said.

"Good deal."

We exchanged a few words before making our way out of the trauma room. As we returned to the ambulance, Ashlee and I discussed how lucky Brett was to have made it through the incident without sustaining any serious injuries.

"It's crazy," Ashlee said. "If that thing had fallen the other direction that would've had an entirely different outcome."

"No kidding," I said. "Hell, you could say he already had 'One foot in the grave.'"

"Oh, lord," Ashlee said, rolling her eyes as she laughed.

"What?" I said, smiling. "Too soon?"

*   *   *

October 2011

It's unrealistic to do this job for any significant amount of time and expect to make it through each call without making mistakes. Obviously, no one *wants* to make a mistake, but it happens. Sometimes, the mistake is made while responding to the scene and an accident happens. Sometimes, a mistake is made during the delivery of treatment. Still, other times the mistake is simply not saying or doing something that you should've said or done. One call in particular always sticks out in the back of my mind that is right up that alley.

It was a cool, late-October afternoon and it had been an especially busy day. Ashlee and I were working together, and Matt was riding with us. He was going through the clearing process to be able to work independently as a paramedic. So far, his clearing process had been pretty uneventful, but all of that was about to change.

"Engine 91, Medic 30, respond to a report of a male subject pinned under a tree."

I looked at Ashlee and said, "Again?"

There had been one fatality already that fall involving a man who had been out cutting trees down. Unfortunately, one of them fell on him, killing him. He was not found until a long time after the accident had happened, but it would not have made a difference if someone had called 911 right when it happened.

"Patient is conscious and breathing," dispatch said over the radio.

"Well that's a plus!" Ashlee said.

"Yeah, better than the last one," I said. I had not been on the call involving the fatality but had heard the details about it. It sounded as if the poor guy was pretty much dead when the limb hit him. Hopefully, I thought, this patient will have a better outcome.

Our response time to the scene was not long. The engine company had made scene several minutes before us, and a BLS ambulance which had freed up was also sent to the call because they were closer. When we arrived at the location, we were met by one of the EMTs from the other ambulance.

"What's the story?" I asked.

"Not good," he said.

"Don't tell me that."

As usual, we grabbed our gear and started walking around the house and into the backyard where the incident location was. The EMT filled me in on the details.

"Looks like he was in the backyard cutting down a tree, but the trunk fell towards him instead of away from him. Sounds like he was pinned for about 10 minutes before his wife came out, found him, and called 911."

"Still conscious?" I inquired.

"Yeah."

As we approached the patient, I noted that he was indeed pinned under a very large tree trunk. It must've been eight or nine feet tall and probably five or six feet around. It had to have weighed 700lbs or so. It was laying perpendicular across the patient's abdominopelvic

75

area. The patient's wife and some neighbors were about 200' away from us, watching from the back porch. Multiple firefighters were surrounding the patient, assessing the situation and devising a plan of action.

"Hey, sir. What's your name?" I asked the patient, attempting to gauge his mental status.

"William."

"William, can you tell me how old you are?"

"Old enough to know better," he said, with obvious pain in his voice.

I thought to myself that it was a good sign that he was able to joke. But joking aside, his situation was dire. The color of his skin was worsening. He was going into shock.

"Mike, Josh, IVs both sides," I asked of two of the firefighters standing there. They immediately complied and went to work starting large bore IVs in William's arms.

"Can we get a bird in the air?" I asked to no one specifically.

Monte, one of the chiefs replied, "Already have one on the way."

Since Matt was the clearing paramedic, he was technically supposed to be running the call, but I think the serious nature of it put me into automatic mode. It was next to impossible for me to stand back and let someone else that was in training call the shots, but nonetheless I tried. I looked over at him and noticed that he looked sort of frozen in his tracks.

"What do you want to do, Matt?"

He looked down at the patient as the wheels in his head turned. He noticed, like I did, that the patient was becoming progressively more lethargic.

"Think we should intubate him?" Matt asked.

"Yeah, he's definitely going to need it," I said.

And with that, Matt knew what he needed to do. He knelt down, opened the jump kits and started getting the necessary equipment and medications ready to perform the intubation. All the while, I was concerned about what would happen when the tree came off of the patient. My primary concern was that the blunt trauma inflicted from the trunk falling on him damaged his internal organs or even his abdominal aorta, and as soon as the pressure being generated from the trunk's positioning was removed, he would rapidly decompensate. Before I could process my next thought, I noticed that the tree was being lifted from the patient. Several of the firefighters decided to come together and lift it off of him by hand. They were able to successfully remove it, and just as I had feared, William stopped breathing. I looked over at the cardiac monitor, which we had placed on him several minutes earlier, and saw that he had gone into full cardiac arrest.

I immediately leaned over and began chest compressions. I looked at Matt and saw that he was still drawing up medications for the intubation. However, now that the patient was in cardiac arrest, we would not need the medications. I think Matt had developed a little tunnel vision with what he was doing and hadn't even noticed we were doing CPR.

"Matt, he's in arrest. We don't need to do the RSI," I said, referring to the procedure of administering medications to facilitate intubation.

Matt made note of the situation and placed the medication vials to the side. He grabbed the laryngoscope and placed it inside William's mouth to attempt an intubation. I could tell he was having a hard time.

"Somebody take over compressions for me, please."

Ashlee, already exhausted from having run back and forth to the ambulance a couple of times for equipment, stepped in and started doing chest compressions. I moved to the patient's head. Matt sat up from his position of looking into William's mouth with the laryngoscope.

"I can't see anything," he said.

"Here, let me give it a shot," I said as I took the laryngoscope from him. I laid on my stomach so I could get the best view possible, inserted the laryngoscope into William's mouth, swept his tongue out of the way with it, and was able to visualize his vocal cords. I took the endotracheal tube and passed it through his cords and then inflated the balloon on the tube that would prevent any air leaks or passage of fluids into his lungs.

"Got it."

"The helicopter is three minutes out," Monte informed me, having received an updated ETA on the radio.

"Might as well tell them to disregard," I said. "They can't fly a CPR-in-progress."

"Okay," Monte said.

We continued doing CPR as we loaded William onto a backboard and then the stretcher. We pushed medications designed to help restart the heart, but they were not having any effect. I could hear

William's wife crying from the porch, her neighbors attempting to console her. Despite excellent compressions being performed by the various firefighters and EMTs on scene, William's color continued to worsen.

"His color is shit," I said.

The poor skin color coupled with the fact that his abdomen appeared to be distending supported my theory that he was bleeding into his abdomen. Most likely, a large portion of his entire blood volume was already in his abdominal and/or pelvic cavity. But we didn't give up. We had to keep trying.

We moved him quickly to the truck. We continued to do chest compressions, continued breathing for him, and continued pushing medications and fluids, but there was no change. His heart rhythm remained flat on the monitor. I called a radio report in to the hospital. The scene of the incident was only about five minutes from the nearest ER. We were there quite quickly.

Once inside the ER, the nurses and doctors worked on William for a good while. When his wife arrived at the ER, one of the nurses asked her if she wanted to come into the trauma room while they were working on him. She did.

I stood outside the room watching through the glass doors as his wife leaned in next to his head, whispering something into his ear. I tried to read her lips but wasn't able to; although, I can imagine what she said to him. Tears streamed down her cheeks, reminders of memories from more than 30 years of marriage.

"You can stop," she said, composing herself just long enough to speak those three words.

The nurse doing chest compressions looked at the doctor. He nodded his head, and she stopped. The monitor tone was a loud, continuous "beeeeeeeeee" as a solid, flat line ran across the heart monitor.

William was pronounced dead.

As I stood there watching William's wife kiss him one last time on the forehead, all I could do was think about what she said to him. And it was then that I regretted the one mistake I made on that call. When I realized that William's condition would deteriorate upon moving the tree, I should have let his wife come down to his side so they could talk to each other for what would've been one last time. They could've looked into each other's eyes one last time. Kissed one last time. Said "I love you" one last time.

But I hadn't thought to do that. And it's one of the few true regrets I carry with me after nearly 20 years in the EMS profession. And it's a mistake I'll never make again should I find myself in a similar situation.

I'm sorry, William. I truly am.

6

O Come, All Ye Faithful

U nlike most people – but not everyone, not by a long shot – EMS providers don't get to take holidays off. EMS is a 24/7/365 service and even though it can be disappointing to miss family functions during the holidays, some truly interesting things can happen during those special times of the year.

*   *   *

December 2009

It's amazing how often you can go for hours at a time without catching a single run, but the second you sit down to eat, the tones go off. A cold December day in 2009 was no different.

My partner, Josh, and I had just sat down to eat and were patiently waiting on our food when the tones were dropped across the radio.

"Medic 30 respond on an unconscious male," the dispatcher directed.

And just as time and time before we got up without our food, exited the restaurant, jumped in the ambulance, and went towards the scene. When we arrived, fire department personnel were already there waiting on us. They had already made an initial assessment of the patient.

"He's pretty lethargic," one of the EMTs reported to me. "But he's breathing normally and sitting in an office chair in the living room."

The residence was in fact a trailer with an unsteady 3-step staircase leading inside. *Typical.* I've had more than one break on me over the years. We made our way carefully up the stairs and into the house where we found our patient. The man was in his 60s, rather heavy set, and bore a striking resemblance to the jolly old elf who'd be delivering presents to kids across the world in just a few days.

The patient's wife was there with him and had been the one to call 911. Upon asking her about what was going on she informed us that he hadn't been feeling well for a couple of days and complained of a headache. She denied any recent injury or illness. He had a history of high blood pressure and diabetes.

Diabetes, I thought. *Perfect. Easy fix.*

If the patient's altered mental status was simply due to low blood sugar we could easily place an IV line and give him intravenous dextrose. We managed to check his blood sugar by poking the tip of his finger to acquire a sample of blood and using our glucometer to check his level. Unfortunately, things were not going to go as easily as I had thought.

His sugar was normal. *Damn.*

The next step was going to be figuring out how to get this large man out of his trailer when the only way in and out was that rickety staircase at the front door. No way can we bring the stretcher in here and risk those stairs collapsing underneath it. We can try to have him walk out. Although he is lethargic and altered he's not completely unconscious. When we would speak to him he'd sort of mumble back to us. It's worth a shot.

I went over to the patient and grabbed his hand and started to pull on him as if to help him up from the seat.

"Come on, buddy," I said. "Let's get you up."

But he wasn't having it. He pulled his hand out of mine and swatted at me, saying nothing in the process. He didn't have to say anything. He made it pretty clear that he wasn't on board with that plan. Time to move on to Plan B.

Plan B was simply rolling the chair over to the front door and attempting to move him down the stairs in the chair. Not the safest plan but we had enough able-bodied men on scene that we should be able to pull it off. That didn't work either. When we attempted to move the chair the patient would start swinging at us. He was simply being defensive. As long as we'd leave him alone, he'd leave us alone. But it was obvious that something was not quite right with him. His wife made that very clear to us.

At this point we're running out of options. We have a large patient whom we are unable to safely remove from the premises in his current state, but we have to get him out of here somehow. I started running through other ideas in my head and about the only thing I could come up with was that we were going to have to sedate him and then would just have to man-handle him out.

I retrieved my controlled substances pouch from the ambulance and removed the vial of midazolam. Midazolam is a potent sedative and is not without risk. But at this point I didn't know what else to do. There's no way I'm going to be able to get an IV on this patient in his current state, but I can give the midazolam via a shot in his arm. My plan was to essentially sneak up behind him, jab it in his arm, and back away before he had the chance to hit me.

And I did just that.

And it only made him more pissed off at us.

He still didn't get up but man oh man did he start swinging and being even more resistant once he felt that needle go in his arm. It'll take a minute or so for the drug to kick in and then he should get sleepy.

But that didn't happen. As a matter of fact his condition didn't change at all. And I had given him a pretty hefty dose.

By this time a sheriff's deputy had arrived. We had called for one not knowing where this was going, but what we did know was that this patient was getting progressively more violent with each attempt we made to get him out of the house. It was in our best interest to have a law enforcement presence.

Unfortunately, the deputy that we received was an older woman with a small frame and short stature. Just a couple of years from retirement. Now don't get me wrong, she was a great deputy and I had worked many scenes with her over the years, but right now what I needed was someone with a gun, a badge, and a lot of muscle.

Steve, I thought to myself.

Steve was a deputy that I had known for years and was a pretty large guy in his own right, but his size came from muscle. I had seen him earlier in the morning when we had breakfast so I knew he was on shift today.

"Can you get Steve up here?" I asked the on-scene deputy.

She got on the radio and contacted him directly requesting that he respond to the scene. He arrived a short time later. While we were waiting for him to arrive I had formulated a new plan. And it was a risky one.

As I've mentioned previously, in addition to the sedatives that we carry on the ambulance (which obviously weren't working), we also carry drugs that literally paralyze you. These paralytics are given, with large doses of sedation as well, to facilitate placing a breathing tube in the windpipe like I described earlier in this book. What I had planned was not really in our protocols, but I figured it was easier to ask for forgiveness than it was to ask for permission. Not something that I would recommend, but sometimes you've got to make stuff up on the fly.

And I was out of options and we had been there for over 2 hours. At this point in time the police were not carrying Tasers. This was the only thing left I could think to do. So I gathered everyone up and explained my plan.

"Here's what we're going to do," I started. "I'm going to come up from behind him with two syringes. In one arm I'm going to inject more sedation and in the other I'm going to inject the paralytic. But the key is, it's going to paralyze everything, including his lungs which means he'll stop breathing."

"I don't know if I like the sound of that," Steve said, rightfully concerned.

"Once it kicks in," I continued, "we'll literally just lay the chair down backwards, slide him up the backboard and I'll be waiting at the head of the board and will intubate him."

"Are you sure this will work?" I was asked.

"That's the general idea," I replied.

We gathered up all of the necessary equipment, checked it to make sure it was working, and set everything up. Behind the chair that the patient was in we set up a backboard on the ground. As soon as he was out, two of the guys would literally tip the chair over backwards onto the ground. They would then slide him up and onto the backboard. On the patient's left side, Kyle, one of the firefighters would put him on the heart monitor and pulse oximeter so we could keep track of his vitals. On the patient's right side was Josh who would be standing by to ventilate the patient with a bag-valve-mask hooked up to oxygen. Lastly, at the head of the patient is where I was going to be, ready and waiting to insert a breathing tube into his throat.

I drew up the medications. More midazolam for sedation and some succinylcholine (SUX) for paralysis. I held the SUX in my right hand and the sedative in my left. I moved towards the patient from behind. Steve stood in front of the patient. Once I was sure everyone was in position and ready I jammed the syringes into either arm and injected the solutions.

The patient immediately began fighting. Steve stepped up on the defensive, holding the patient down in his seat.

"You're strong," Steve said. "But I'm stronger!"

The patient was a good match for Steve and they pushed against each other like the same ends of two magnets when you try and push them together. But then the paralytics kicked in and the patient went limp. Steve was still pushing against the patient when the medication took affect and actually ended up falling into him which led to the chair tipping over backwards. The firefighters that were in place caught the chair and lowered the patient safely to the ground.

Everybody was doing exactly what they were assigned to do. The patient was moved up the backboard. Kyle placed the patient on the heart monitor and the pulse oximeter. Unfortunately, the patient's heart rate was noted to be quite low (in the 30s) as was his oxygen level. Most likely the patient had used up his oxygen while struggling with the deputy.

I ordered Josh to ventilate the patient and told Kyle to start chest compressions. Although the patient still had a pulse he needed a little pick-me-up. I leaned over and placed the laryngoscope into the patient's mouth. As I was doing this I remember the female deputy expressing some concern.

"Have you done this before?!" she asked.

Although I had performed the procedure several times during my career I had not exactly done it in these circumstances. I thought it best to just ignore her inquiry.

I inserted the breathing tube, verified placement, and secured it in place. With the added oxygen his vital signs returned to normal without further incident. I placed an IV and gave him additional sedation to make sure he stayed asleep.

We secured the patient to the backboard, scooted it over to the front door, and then moved it out the front door and onto the stretcher. Transport to the hospital was uneventful and he remained stable. Once we arrived there we took him into the trauma room where we were greeted by the doctor and the nursing team. I told them what we encountered on scene and what we chose to do for treatment.

"You're brave," the doctor commented, referring to the tactics I chose to utilize.

I'm not really sure if it was bravery, stupidity, or a combination of both. A lot of things could've gone wrong on that call and almost did. But in the end it worked out and we were able to safely transport the patient to the hospital where he was eventually diagnosed with encephalitis before being treated and released back to home to enjoy the holidays.

I still look back on that run and think that that's the year we saved Santa Claus.

*   *   *

December 2016

"Stand down from your transfer," the dispatcher's voice crackled across the radio. "We need you to divert to a scene flight. Train vs. car. Subject is unresponsive."

The aircraft banked to the right as the course heading was adjusted.

"How far out are we?" I asked over the cockpit headset system.

"Just a couple of minutes," replied the pilot.

We had been on our way to a small community hospital to transport a patient with a heart condition to a larger hospital which specialized in cardiac conditions when we received the order to reroute to the scene of the train/car accident. We were only a few minutes from the scene. My partner, a flight nurse, and I had been working together for several months and had developed a good working relationship and routine. We already knew what to expect from each other when we arrived on the scene.

Before we knew it we were circling over the scene of the accident. It didn't look good. A minivan had been struck by a train on the passenger side and pushed a good distance down the tracks. Fire, police, and EMS crews were already on the scene and I could tell they were standing at the driver's side. We did a quick recon of the area to make sure there were no obstructions or hazards that would make landing dangerous. Once we cleared the area we landed in a field about 100 yards from the scene.

We grabbed our gear and started the short hike across the field. I made it to the side of the vehicle first. The fire department paramedic was standing at the side of the patient placing an IO needle into his upper arm. I shifted my attention to the patient. His shirt was saturated in blood which appeared to be coming from his mouth, nose, and ears. That isn't good.

"Is he breathing?" I asked of the unconscious man.

The fire department medic looked over his shoulder at me and shook his head. I immediately motioned to my partner to get our BVM from our equipment bag so we could deliver artificial ventilations to the patient.

"Does he have a pulse?" was my follow-up question to which the medic also replied "No."

"Well we need to get him out of there then," I suggested.

Generally speaking, resuscitation is not attempted in the field on patients who have suffered a cardiac arrest from blunt trauma. The chances of successful resuscitation and survival are extremely low. Patients who have arrested secondary to penetrating trauma have a slightly higher chance of survival but that's typically if a trauma surgeon can perform life-saving surgery on them quickly. Why the difference?

Well, imagine taking a baseball bat to a pumpkin; the pumpkin is smashed into dozens of pieces which would be nearly impossible to return to normal. That's blunt trauma. Now imagine taking a knife and stabbing a hole through a pumpkin. That's penetrating trauma. In theory, it's much easier to plug the hole than it is to put all of the broken pieces back together. Right? Of course it's also important to keep in mind what structures on the other side of the hole were damaged by the penetrating object.

The area we were in was a small rural community where everybody knows everybody. Family members of the injured man had already made it to the scene and were watching attentively. We decided to give it a try. The patient was rapidly removed from the car whose driver's side door had already been taken off. Positioning him on a backboard, we carried him up a small hill to the fire department's ambulance.

Our rapid assessment revealed significant head trauma but otherwise no obvious injuries. We did what we always do with these patients; we did CPR, started IVs, gave fluids, intubated and gave him breaths. His heart rhythm remained in asystole. With each compression more blood came out of his mouth and even up through the breathing tube – a sign of significant chest trauma/bleeding in the chest. We worked on him for about 10 minutes and then had a discussion that probably should've been had at the very beginning; whether or not to terminate resuscitation efforts. I took my phone out and called our medical director – the physician who oversees what we do as medical providers.

After speaking to him and painting a picture of the patient's condition and the treatment we had provided he agreed with our decision to halt all efforts at resuscitating the man. At that point we stopped CPR and it was over; he was dead. I looked up from the patient and out the back window where I saw a group of people consoling each other…family. Someone had to tell them.

Telling someone that their loved one has died is never an easy thing to do, but like most things in this line of work it gets easier to do with time. Unfortunately, I had had to have these kinds of conversations several times in the past. It was almost a script I had developed for these situations.

I'm sorry for your loss.

It appears it was quick.

He probably didn't feel anything.

These are the things you say to make them feel better; as better as someone can feel who just lost a loved one I guess. Most of the time they know their loved one is gone before you tell them, but when you say those words it becomes official. It all ends. All of the good times, the bad times, the memory-making, the phone calls, the text messages, the holidays and birthdays spent together, the hugs and kisses, the "goodnights," and the "see you tomorrows." In the blink of an eye. Just…gone.

I made my way from the ambulance to the group of people standing in the middle of the street. They had arrived there even before we did. They'd seen us remove his lifeless body from the wreckage, seen us thumping on his chest. They knew it was bad and yet the expressions on their faces still displayed a glimmer of hope; blind optimism.

"Are you family?" I asked, even though I already knew.

"Yes. I'm his daughter," one young woman replied.

She was a petite brunette, probably no older than her early thirties. I could tell she had just thrown on some clothes, probably whatever was laying around her room when her phone rang.

"As you guys know he was seriously injured in the accident. You could probably see him when we removed him from the car," I said.

She nodded, sniffling.

"When we got to him he had no heart beat and was not breathing. We put a tube in his windpipe so we could breathe for him, did CPR, and gave him medicine to try and restart his heart. But unfortunately, it appears the injuries he sustained were just too severe. He didn't respond to any of our treatment," I explained.

As I spoke, I could see what little hope she was holding on to slowly disappear. Her eyes started to swell and water.

"And I'm very sorry to have to tell you, but he has died," I said, very clearly.

You're taught from the beginning to never sugarcoat it or use phrases like "he's gone" or "he's no longer with us." Family members are often in a state of shock during this time and need to hear clear, concise words.

"Can I see him?" she asked.

"Of course," I replied.

I informed her I would need a minute to clean him up a bit and then I would let her spend as much time with him as she wanted. I returned to the ambulance and informed my partner and the EMS crew that the daughter would be coming to see her father and asked them to clean him up a bit as he was covered in blood. The IVs and breathing tube would have to stay in due to the nature of his death and it becoming a coroner's case. I walked back to the group of family and friends. I explained to the daughter what she would see once we reached the ambulance. I wanted her to be prepared.

As we approached the ambulance, I offered a reassuring arm around her shoulders and told her to let me know if she had any questions. We reached the side door of the ambulance and she looked at her dead father laying on the stretcher. She was no longer able to hold back her tears.

"Daddy!" she cried out.

Daddy.

She stepped into the ambulance and lightly slid her fingers across his face.

"I'm so sorry," she said softly.

She leaned over and kissed him on the forehead, stood up, sniffled, wiped her tears away, and looked at all of us.

"Thank you," she said before turning and stepping out of the ambulance.

None of the other family members wanted to see him at the moment. I walked the daughter back to her loved ones and informed her about what would be happening with the body. I asked if she had any questions for me. She didn't. I apologized to her for her loss and welcomed a hug that she offered to me.

The group thanked me again. They *thanked* me. It didn't seem right. We didn't succeed. But we did try. Maybe that was enough for them. I hope so. I stood there and watched as they walked back towards the vehicle, embracing each other.

Christmas Eve would never be the same for them again.

*   *   *

December 2010

It seemed like it was taking forever. The other drivers on the road were doing a decent job getting out of our way, but it still seemed like it was taking longer than it should. It was New Year's Eve, and we were trying desperately to get to a residence where a fourteen year old boy had been accidentally shot in the abdomen following a hunting outing with a friend.

We finally made it to the house which was located out in the country. People move to the countryside for several reasons. They enjoy the isolation, the peace and quiet, and the space between neighbors. But the decision to move further away from town just increases the time it takes for responders to make it to you if someone is hurt, your house is on fire, or there is an intruder. When we arrived on scene, the fire and police departments were already there. We were directed to the back of the house by a sheriff's deputy.

When I made entry into the home I was presented with a young boy, awake and obviously scared. A firefighter was kneeling down beside him holding a trauma dressing to his abdomen. It was soaked in blood. The boy was incredibly pale. It was difficult to tell how much blood had already been lost but it appeared to be significant. I immediately told one of the firefighters to request a medical helicopter for transport to the children's trauma center which was easily more than an hour and a half away by ground. I gently pulled back the trauma dressing to try and visualize the wound. Blood began spurting.

94

Shit. It's an arterial wound.

Wounds to arteries can be disastrous because arterial blood flow is under high pressure. A human can bleed out in just a couple of minutes from an arterial injury.

The boy was currently awake but was getting lethargic. An altered level of consciousness in a trauma patient is an ominous sign. We quickly packaged him onto a backboard and moved him to the ambulance. I had already made the decision in my head that I was going to intubate him. His condition was deteriorating and I wanted to get ahead of it the best I could so I wanted to secure his airway. It would be one less thing I had to worry about. I asked two of the EMTs on scene to start IVs on either side of his body; they quickly handled the task.

Meanwhile, I was drawing up the medications that I would need to properly sedate and paralyze him. His father climbed into the back of the ambulance and was consoling him.

I looked at the boy and explained to him that we were going to be putting him to sleep and that he'd be waking up at the children's hospital in the best hands possible.

"Am I going to be okay?" he asked.

"We're doing everything we can," I said. In reality, I wasn't sure what his prognosis was. He had lost a lot of blood, and his leg looked as if the circulation to it was compromised.

"Alright, buddy. Here we go," I said before pushing the induction medications.

Shortly after administering the medications, the boy's body started to display muscle fasciculations which is a phenomenon known to occur occasionally with these types of medications. The fasciculations, which are muscle twitches, can resemble seizure activity to the untrained eye.

"Is that supposed to happen?" his dad asked.

"It can happen sometimes. He'll be okay," I reassured him.

We completed the procedure without any complications. It was shortly after that that I could hear what was music to my ears: the helicopter. The medevac helicopter landed in a nearby field and the flight nurse and flight paramedic made their way to the ambulance.

I gave them a report of the patient's condition and the treatment we had provided thus far. We tightened down the pressure dressing that was controlling the bleeding from the wound site and then packaged him onto their stretcher, helped load him into the aircraft and then moved away to a safe distance.

The engines powered up and the rotor blades spun faster. Debris from the field shot out from underneath the multi-million dollar machine as it lifted from the ground. Higher into the air it went before turning to the northeast and taking off towards the children's hospital. I looked on as I always did when I would land a helicopter at a scene.

That is such a cool gig.

That's what I want to do.

Several months after the accident I had the opportunity to meet with the patient and his family. They were a great group of people, so appreciative of our actions that cold December morning. They explained to us how at one point he was in danger of possibly losing his leg, but luckily the doctors were able to save it and, more importantly, save him. His family told us that the ER doctors explained that if it wasn't for our ability to control that massive arterial bleed, and our decision to fly him to the pediatric trauma center, the outcome may have been very different.

To this day when I see his family out in public we say hello to each other, and I'll give him a pat on the shoulder. He's in his 20s now, a grown man, and it's a good feeling to know that I was part of the team that made sure he got that chance to grow up.

7

The Heart of the Matter

Without a doubt calls involving heart problems are some of the most common types of medical emergencies we respond to. Sometimes these calls end up being nothing more than simple chest pain (without an actual heart attack), but other times they end up being something more.

*　　*　　*

May 2006

The sun was slowly starting to peek out above the horizon, bringing light to a new day. Birds were chirping and roosters were crowing, but one loud noise was drowning out those peaceful sounds of nature...our siren. It was just after six in the morning and we were on our way to a "heart problems" call at a private residence. The address was located a decent distance out in the countryside. The view was breath-taking as the sunrise lit up the green grass fields and freshly blooming trees.

We pulled up in front of the mailbox and into the driveway which went back a long way from the road; so long that we couldn't see the house from our current position. We made our way down the drive and found the house, nestled within a cluster of large trees. It was a gorgeous two-story home hidden within their own small piece of paradise. My partner and I exchanged looks with each other, neither of us having ever been in a home this nice before.

We pulled the stretcher from the back of the ambulance, placed the cardiac monitor and equipment bag on it and walked up to the front door where a woman in her 50s was waiting for us.

"Good morning, ma'am."

She flashed a forced smile at us as she motioned us inside.

"He's in here," she said as she led us to the living room.

It was difficult to not look all around their house as we walked through the kitchen and dining room and into the living room. It was impeccably clean. Family photos lined the walls of the hallway and a shrine dedicated to the sport of golf made it clear what the husband's favorite hobby was.

As we entered the living room we were met with the patient, Paul, who was sitting on the couch in a robe.

"Good morning, sir. What's going on today?" I asked.

"Well, two weeks ago I had a heart catherization done because I've been having episodes of chest pain pretty frequently over the last month or so. The doctor put a stent in and I've been doing pretty well. But this morning while I was walking on the treadmill I developed this heavy pressure right here," he explained as he pointed to his upper left chest. "I got a little dizzy too, so I stopped walking and sat down."

"Did you take anything for the pain?"

"Yes. I took two nitro and an aspirin."

"Did it help?"

"Yeah. I can barely tell anything's wrong now. I told my wife not to call you guys, but she didn't listen. She worries a lot," he said as he flashed his wife a smile. "I really don't think I need to go to the hospital. I'm feeling much better now."

"Well I can certainly understand your desire to not go to the hospital, but I think that your recent heart history coupled with the fact that you had this pressure while you were exercising is cause for caution," I said before adding, "And the fact that the nitroglycerin relieved your pain raises my suspicions even more that it was in fact caused by a potential heart problem. I can't say that with 100% certainty, but it's a pretty good bet."

"Honey, why don't you just go in and get checked out," his wife asked of him.

I could tell that Paul was conflicted over the idea of going to the hospital and it was obvious that his wife was quite concerned for his wellbeing and wanted him to go. She wanted us to just make him go but a lot of people don't understand that we just can't make patients go against their will. There are only a very few specific circumstances when we can take a patient against his or her wishes. This was not one of them.

It took a few more minutes of convincing, but Paul finally consented to transport. We secured him to the stretcher and loaded him in the ambulance; his wife would follow in her personal car. As we began transport, I obtained an ECG of his heart; it appeared normal. At this point Paul was stating that he no longer had pressure and was now complaint-free. I inserted an IV, drew some blood, and put him on a little bit of oxygen via a nasal cannula. Since he was no longer symptomatic it was pretty much just transport and observe, so I began working on my run sheet.

We were about 8-10 minutes away from the hospital when suddenly all of the color drained from Paul's face.

"I feel nauseous," he said.

He seemed as if he might lose consciousness.

"I think you're going to lose me," he said.

I instantly became extremely worried about him. One thing that you're taught earlier in your EMS training is that if a patient thinks they are going to die, believe them!

I looked down at the cardiac monitor and noticed that Paul's heart rate had dropped significantly. He had had a rate in the 70s but now was only showing a rate in the 20s-30s. I immediately lowered the head of the stretcher so Paul was lying flat and yelled up to my partner,

"Mike, step it up!"

Mike turned on the lights and siren in order to expedite our trip to the ER.

I reached for the medication atropine. Atropine can be used for a couple of different things including increasing a slow heart rate. Sometimes it works, sometimes it doesn't. As I was getting the medication out of the box I kept talking to Paul to try and keep him awake. He was very lethargic and distressed. I removed the medication from the box, prepped it for administration and hooked it up to his IV line, pushing the end of the vial to inject the medication fluid through the medication port in the IV tubing.

"Hang in there, Paul. I just gave you some medication to try and turn this around," I said.

While I was waiting to see if he responded to the medication I began to take out our defibrillation pads. Before I could get them placed on Paul's chest the heart monitor showed a steady increase in his heart rate. His rate increased to about 100 beats per minute and was strong and regular. The color in his face was returning to normal. His level of consciousness dramatically improved as well.

"What happened?" he asked.

"I'm not real sure, Paul. Your heart rate dropped to a dangerously low level. I gave you some medicine to speed it back up. I'm not sure why it dropped though."

I ran a second ECG but it was the same as the first one; there had been no acute changes surprisingly. Paul's blood pressure, which had dropped significantly due to the low heart rate, was also returning to normal. I breathed a sigh of relief. That was close. The remaining five minutes of the transport was uneventful. Paul remained stable and had no further changes in his condition. When we arrived at the hospital, as we were removing him from the ambulance, he looked over at me.

"Let's not tell my wife about this," he said.

The meaning behind his comment stuck with me for a good while. Despite him having thought that he was about to die in the back of my ambulance, the first thing that goes through his mind is to not worry his wife any more than she already was by telling her what happened. Even when he thought he was near death his first concern was for the wellbeing of his wife.

We took Paul into the ER and transferred care to the ER staff so they could continue taking care of him. His wife walked into the room shortly after we moved him to the bed.

"How was the ride?" she asked Paul.

"Just fine," he said, looking at me with a grin as Mike and I walked out of the room.

*   *   *

June 2008

It seemed like the rain would never end. I couldn't remember the last time that I had seen it rain so heavily for such an extended period of time. It didn't take long before the National Weather Service was issuing flash flood warnings for the area. Evacuations were ordered for certain neighborhoods and even some nursing homes needed to be cleared out. We hadn't seen flooding like that in our area for 100 years or so.

Luckily, I was actually out of town when the rain first came. I was having Lasik done and my friend and I were not able to get home on the first night because the main roads home were flooded out, and we didn't want to risk taking the back roads and finding ourselves being washed away. So we decided to get a hotel and make the drive home the next morning.

When we got back in town the next day I was taken aback by the amount of damage that had been done. My own grandfather had to be removed from his apartment by a water rescue team. I went to work not knowing what kinds of problems I'd run into that were related to these flood waters, but it wouldn't be long before I found out.

Lois was a sweet lady, somewhere in her 60s. She lived at home with her husband where they both enjoyed a quiet retirement. But on this particular weekend there was nothing quiet or peaceful about their lives. For the last 24 hours they had been keeping a close watch on a nearby creek that had quickly risen above its banks. The water had essentially created a moat around their home, and there was no getting in or out of their property with the little town car they owned.

Lois found herself feeling pretty anxious over the rising water, but she suddenly began to feel something more than mere anxiety. While standing in the kitchen washing the dishes she was suddenly overcome with dizziness and nausea almost to the point where she felt like she might pass out.

She called out to her husband who helped her into their bedroom so she could lay down. But the symptoms didn't go away. In fact, they only got worse. Even while lying in her bed Lois felt like the room was spinning and her husband became even more concerned when she told him she felt like her heart was racing and she couldn't catch her breath. Her husband realized that they needed help so he called 911.

"Rescue 21, Tac-41, Medic 30, respond to a female with heart problems. May also require a water rescue," the dispatcher announced over the radio.

While en route to the scene we were able to obtain some additional information. We learned that the patient's house was completely surrounded by water and the driveway leading up to their residence was flooded as well. Tac-41 was the county's water rescue team at the time but it was stationed on the opposite side of the county from where Lois lived; their response time was going to be lengthy.

When we arrived on the scene it was clear to us that the information we had received was indeed accurate and we were not going to be able to get the ambulance up to the house. We were met by a member of the local volunteer fire department who informed us that other members of the department were already inside the home with the patient. They had been transported through the high waters in the back of a neighbor's truck, and he was on his way back to get us.

We gathered up our equipment while we waited for the truck to get back to us. When it arrived, we climbed into the bed and began the 3 minute journey through the woods and water to get to the house. Once we arrived at the residence we jumped from the back of the truck and made our way inside where we were directed to a back bedroom.

We found Lois still in bed and not looking well. Her skin was pale and slightly clammy and she looked quite uncomfortable.

"Hello, ma'am. My name's Chris, I'm a paramedic. What's going on today?"

"I'm terribly dizzy," Lois said. "I can't stand up without feeling like I might pass out."

I knelt down and felt for her radial pulse as I continued asking questions.

"Are you having any chest pain?"

She shook her head.

"It's more like I feel like my heart is trying to jump out of my chest."

I was unable to feel her radial pulse. *Not good.* I looked over at one of the EMTs from the fire department.

"Blood pressure?"

"I'm only getting about 70 systolic," the EMT replied.

"How's your breathing, Lois?" I asked.

"It's OK," she replied, although it was obvious she seemed a little winded.

While my partner placed our blood pressure cuff on Lois's arm I began to hook her up to our cardiac monitor.

"Do you have a history of any heart problems?" I asked.

"No. Just high blood pressure and diabetes."

I gathered some additional information about her medical history while I finished hooking her up to the heart monitor. Once she was on it and the rhythm was displayed on the screen it was obvious why she felt the way she did.

Her heart rate was 230.

The normal resting heart rate for an adult should be, on average, in the 70s. But Lois had a dysrhythmia known as supraventricular tachycardia (SVT). There are a few different kinds of SVT and some have more specific names. In general, SVT is a dysrhythmia that originates somewhere in the heart above the ventricles (the lower chambers of the heart) and has a heart rate greater than 100. The faster the rate is the more concerning the situation, primarily because the patient's cardiac output (amount of blood pumped out of the heart) is diminished and thus their blood pressure drops as we were seeing with Lois.

There are several different dysfunctions that can lead to an SVT dysrhythmia, and we do carry medications on the ambulance that can help restore the rhythm to a normal rate but not without a degree of risk. My partner had obtained a blood pressure of 78/46 and coupled with Lois's verbalized complaints and the findings of her physical assessment it was obvious that there was cardiac compromise, and we needed to terminate the dysrhythmia immediately.

106

The severity of her presentation made her a candidate for immediate synchronized cardioversion: shocking her with the defibrillator to terminate the SVT and essentially "reset" her conduction system. I chose not to go that route though because I did not have our sedatives with me; they were locked up in the ambulance, and I did not want to shock this little old lady without first sedating her. I decided to give the medications a shot first. Medicine before Edison.

By this time I had already placed an IV in her and was drawing up the medication adenosine. Adenosine works by blocking atrioventricular (AV) node conduction and typically terminates about 90% of these types of rhythms. I had yet to see it fail. The trick with adenosine is that its efficacy is very short-lived so you have to get it to the heart quickly. We do this by administering it rapidly and following it with a rapid flush of IV fluids.

The protocol for administration of the adenosine was to give 6mg for the first dose with the option to repeat at 12mg two additional times. While I was drawing up the first 6mg into a syringe I explained the plan to Lois and informed her that the medication would most likely make her feel quite funny. After all, when you are watching the heart monitor after giving adenosine you'll actually see the patient's heart "flat-line" for a short interval. That always causes your butt to pucker a little because there's always a chance that it might not start back up.

I placed the adenosine syringe on one of the IV ports and the saline flush on the other port. I quickly pushed the adenosine syringe in and chased it with the saline. I then had the EMT holding the bag of saline squeeze it to push in even more fluids. And then I watched the monitor screen and waited.

It seemed like it was taking forever. I checked the IV site to make sure the IV had not blown. It was patent. Then I saw the look on Lois's face and could tell she was feeling its effects. I turned my attention back to the monitor and sure enough the rhythm was slowing down before flat-lining, as expected. It only lasted a brief moment before normal complexes started again. I was pleased that it had worked. But then quickly realized that the rate was climbing. And climbing. And climbing. Before I knew it the rate was all the way back up at 250. The medication had failed.

That's OK, I thought. That happens from time to time. That's why the protocol allows for three doses. So I drew up 12mg and repeated the process.

Same results.

Another 12mg.

Nothing.

At this point it was obvious that we were going to have to cardiovert Lois if we were hoping to break the rhythm. But I wasn't going to do it without sedation, so we needed to get her back to the ambulance which means we're going to have to go off-roading again since we couldn't get the ambulance to her.

We had one option at this point. We had to get Lois into that truck and make our way back to the ambulance. Without having the stretcher the only way we could transport her to the truck was with a backboard.

We secured Lois to a backboard and made her as comfortable as we could. We secured the monitor in place so we could keep an eye on the rhythm and her blood pressure. We carried her out of the house and slid the backboard into the back of the pickup truck. My partner and I climbed into the back and stayed by Lois's side as we slowly made our way back to the ambulance.

Once we cleared the flood waters, we pulled Lois out of the back of the truck and moved her to the stretcher, removing the backboard in the process. We loaded her into the truck and prepared for the cardioversion procedure.

While my partner placed the defibrillation pads on Lois's chest I removed our controlled substances pouch from the locked compartment where we kept them and removed the midazolam. Midazolam is a good choice for a situation like this because not only does it sedate the patient but it also has amnesia properties so the patient won't remember what happened. It does have to be used with caution though because it can cause a drop in blood pressure and Lois's pressure was already low.

I drew up the medication and prepared to administer it. I explained to Lois that she was going to feel like she was kicked in the chest by a horse, but that it was going to solve the problem (hopefully). I also told her that she wouldn't remember any of it (again, hopefully).

She was anxious, rightfully so. I placed an oxygen mask on her face and administered the sedative. After a moment, it kicked in and she was out. I reached over to the monitor and charged it.

As I listened to the familiar sound of the monitor charging up I felt a little nervous. This was the first time in 3 years as a paramedic that I had to cardiovert someone. Every patient I had in the past with a similar problem had responded quickly to the medications. But not Lois. She was making us earn our money today.

I had defibrillated dozens of people over the years who were in cardiac arrest, but this was the first time that I'd have to shock a live patient. But she needed it and it was time to do it. The monitor was fully charged and it was time to press the "shock" button.

And I did.

And she screamed.

And then it was over.

The cardioversion worked like a charm. The dysrhythmia resolved and her heart was now beating normally. Her blood pressure instantly improved as expected. Although Lois's scream was quite loud when the shock hit her, she was already fast asleep. Her husband, who had ridden in the front seat of the pick-up truck, heard the screaming from inside the ambulance and was looking through the back window. I opened the door so he could see her.

"She's okay," I assured him. "The shock worked and her heart is back to normal. She'll be asleep for a little while because of the sedative we gave her."

He climbed into the front of the ambulance to ride to the hospital with us. On the way there I kept an eye on Lois's heart as well as her breathing. She did just fine during the 20 minute trip to the ER. No changes.

Once at the ER we transferred her to the exam room bed and I gave report to the receiving RN. We cleaned the truck and finished up our paperwork. I went back to Lois's room before we left to check on her and found that she was finally waking up. She looked amazingly better. Her skin was normal in color and the monitor next to her bed displayed a normal heart rate and blood pressure.

"I'm glad to see you're doing better," I said. "Hopefully we didn't hurt you too much."

"Well I don't know. The last thing I remember is you saying that I wouldn't remember anything," Lois said with a laugh and a grateful smile.

*   *   *

April 2011

It's often said that one of the factors of public safety jobs that keeps workers coming back is that no two calls are the same. And in all honesty I've spoken those words myself from time to time when I'm asked what it is I love about my job. But the reality is that a lot of the time calls *are* the same. Sure, you meet different people and go to different places, but belly pain is belly pain and a broken leg is a broken leg. However, every once and a while you get a reminder about why you should never be complacent in this line of work. My run-in with Eugene was one of those reminders.

Eugene was a 72 year old gentleman who lived at home with his wife. They had been married for 50 years and during that time had faced a lot of challenges but nothing would compare to the events that would unfold on the day that our paths crossed.

It was a warm summer day, and the call volume had been relatively light so far. My partner, Heather, and I were just finishing up lunch when that familiar sound of our tones broke the silence from our radio.

"Medic 30, respond to a report of a 69 year old male with heart problems," the dispatcher said.

While we were en route to the scene we were provided with further information. The caller had advised that her husband has a pacemaker/defibrillator and it had shocked him twice. He was conscious and breathing but was in pain.

111

I had been on countless "defib firing" calls by this point in my career; all of them amounted to not much more than obtaining an ECG and transporting the patient to the hospital. I expected nothing more than just that with this particular call as well.

The address of the residence was easy to find as the street they lived on was right around the corner from my own house. We pulled up in front of it and behind the fire engine which was already on scene. We grabbed our heart monitor, unloaded the stretcher and made our way inside the house.

Once inside the house we found Eugene sitting in a recliner in the living room. He didn't appear particularly distressed. He was quite overweight though. His wife was standing by in the adjoining kitchen with a couple of concerned neighbors who came over after seeing the fire engine parked out front. As I stepped closer to Eugene to begin my assessment my attention was immediately drawn to the engine company's heart monitor. My level of concern as it related to the patient quickly increased. The rhythm displayed on the monitor was ventricular tachycardia, or V-Tach.

V-Tach is a potentially deadly cardiac dysrhythmia which if left untreated could easily lead to cessation of heart contractions. I asked the firefighter/EMTs if they had obtained a blood pressure and they advised that they had not been able to. Not surprising. I stepped over to Eugene, knelt down and felt for the radial pulse at his wrist. I was able to count one heart beat in a 30 second timespan which basically meant he had a palpable pulse of 2 per minute. He was completely awake and alert complaining only of slight chest pain from when his internal defibrillator had shocked him. Twice.

"Heather, get our drug box right now," I said.

While Heather went out to retrieve our drug box I removed the defibrillation pads from the monitor and placed them on the patient's chest. I asked him a few questions while I started an IV in his right hand. I drew up the antidysrhythmic drug lidocaine which has the potential to terminate the lethal rhythm. I pushed the medication through the IV line, and then I watched and waited.

I looked on as the monitor continued to display V-Tach. No change. Not even a brief hiccup. It wasn't working. The next thing to do to break the rhythm is to perform synchronized cardioversion. This was not something I wanted to do to him while he was sitting in his recliner. That's the last place I wanted him to be if he would actually end up going into cardiac arrest. We needed to get him onto the stretcher. He was much too large for us to pick up so we helped him stand and move to the stretcher.

Bad idea.

Although moving him only required him standing up, turning around, and sitting back down that was enough to put him into arrest. His cardiac function was already so poor that even the slightest bit of exertion pushed him over the edge. He went unresponsive and we lost his pulse.

"Start compressions," I advised the firefighter closest to his chest. He began pumping on Eugene's chest.

I looked over at the monitor and saw that the patient was still in V-Tach. *Good,* I thought. At least that still gives us something to work with. As I reached over to the monitor to charge it the other firefighters got Eugene's legs up on the stretcher. And then suddenly something caught my attention.

Groans.

113

With each compression a telltale groan was coming from Eugene. I looked up towards his head and saw that the grey color that had washed over his body was quickly transitioning to pink.

"Hold compressions," I said as I directed my attention back to the heart monitor.

It was back into a normal rhythm.

Eugene started coming around rather quickly. We sat the head of the stretcher up.

"Are you with us, Eugene?" I asked.

"Yeah," he answered, groggy. "What happened?"

"You gave us a bit of a scare for a minute, but you're doing better now."

We placed an oxygen mask on him and finished securing him to the stretcher. As Heather and the firefighters took him outside to the ambulance I stepped over to speak to Eugene's wife who had been watching in terror from the adjacent kitchen. She was sitting on one of the dining table chairs with a neighbor at her side. I sat down in a chair across from her.

"He's doing okay," I said. "Obviously you saw us have to do chest compressions on him, but his heart rhythm has returned to normal. We're going to take him to the hospital and see if they can figure out what happened and why his defibrillator wasn't able to break the rhythm."

"Thank you so much," she said.

"We'll take good care of him," I assured her.

As we loaded him into the ambulance I started thinking through what had happened and what most likely caused his heart to return to a normal rhythm without us having actually cardioverted him. The lidocaine that I had given him probably did not work as quickly as expected because of how poor his cardiac output was. When we started doing chest compressions the medication was actually able to be circulated and was able to terminate the arrhythmia. I couldn't say for sure, but it made sense.

Once in the ambulance I initiated a lidocaine infusion to help prevent any recurrence of the V-Tach. The 15 minute trip to the hospital was otherwise uneventful. Eugene was back to normal and feeling better. His vital signs were right where they should be, and his ECG showed no signs of heart attack or other abnormalities.

We arrived at the ER and took him into Trauma 3. I gave my report to the nurses and one of them, Josh, high-fived me for the positive outcome. Kind of silly, sure, but also a definitive feel-good moment. The man had literally been dead in front of us one minute and the next he was awake and talking.

It's true that having him exert himself to move to the stretcher undoubtedly led to the arrest, but at the time there was no other way to move him due to his size. As they say, hindsight is 20/20 and since then I approach similar situations differently.

A previous medical director of mine would always say, "They call it 'practicing medicine' for a reason: because we are practicing our craft when we treat patients in hopes of one day being perfect at it."

He's not wrong.

Practice does make perfect.

Or at least something close to it.

- 8 -

Grace on Wings

It's a common occurrence when one works in the medical field to find a mentor that they look up to, learn from, and go to when they have questions about something. I was lucky enough to have several mentors help me during my formative years, but there was one doctor in particular that stands out when I look back.

*   *   *

July 2011

The morning started like any typical Monday morning. We clocked in, checked off the equipment on our ambulance, signed out our drugs, and left our station to get some breakfast. Before we could make it to the restaurant of our choice we were dispatched to respond to a motor vehicle accident with minor injuries. As usual, breakfast would have to wait.

The accident scene was located about three minutes from the hospital and was indeed minor. More of a fender bender than anything; however, there was one patient who was requesting transport for ankle pain. It was one of those patients where you can't help but wonder if they're really hurt or if they're just faking it in order to go after a payout from the other driver's insurance company. Regardless, they make the complaint and we take it seriously. The ankle in question did not have any obvious trauma to it but we went ahead and splinted it and placed an ice pack on it for good measure. We had just loaded the stretcher back into the ambulance when my phone started ringing. I pulled it out of my pocket to silence it and saw that it was my father that was calling. It struck me as odd that he would be calling me at 7:30 in the morning; that's very unusual but nevertheless I had a patient and couldn't answer it at that exact moment. I sent the call to voicemail.

After performing an assessment on the patient and determining that they did not require advanced life support-level care, I deferred the rest of the patient's care to my EMT partner and got out of the ambulance to drive us to the hospital. Once we left the scene I called my father back.

"What's up?" I asked when he answered the phone.

"Are you working today?" he asked.

"Yes."

"Do you think you could come by and look at Linda and let me know if you think she should go to the hospital?"

Linda is my step-mother and at the time was dealing with a lot of various health issues.

"What's wrong with her?" I inquired.

"I'm not sure. I'm just having a hard time waking her up," he replied with a concerned tone in his voice.

I informed him that I was transporting a patient to the ER but would be at the hospital in about a minute. We would drop off the patient and then head over to his house which was about a seven or eight minute drive from the ER. I asked him if she was breathing normally and after he assured me she was I ended the call as we pulled into the ambulance bay at the hospital.

We dropped off the patient and gave report to the receiving RN. Due to the minor nature of the patient's injuries, transfer of care took place pretty quickly. I informed my partner, Ashlee, about the phone call with my dad and told her I would call dispatch to let them know we'd be going over there.

We quickly got the stretcher back together, the back of the ambulance cleaned up, and headed towards my father's house. My gut was telling me that there was something bad going on and by this time in my career I had learned to trust my gut. I flipped on the lights and siren to get there fast. We pulled up in front of their residence a few minutes later. I didn't even think to grab any equipment before I ran inside; I just shifted the truck into park and ran up to the front door.

My father was waiting at the front door and held it open for me, directing me to the couch just inside the entry. I stepped in and looked down to see Linda laying there, apparently unconscious. The first thing that I noticed was her color; she was ashen. An ashen appearance in a patient is often an indication of low oxygen levels. I also made note of the fact that although her respiratory rate was near twenty, her breaths were very shallow. A normal respiratory rate for an adult is between 12 and 20, but if she wasn't taking deep enough breaths there was no way she was getting enough oxygen into her system.

I stepped over to her side, saying her name as I approached her. She didn't respond. I proceeded to do a sternal rub to see if I could illicit a painful response; it worked. She moaned in pain. Next, I removed my stethoscope from around my neck to listen to her lungs and found that my suspicions were correct; she had little to no air movement throughout her lung fields.

Ashlee stepped inside with our pulse oximeter – a device that measures the amount of oxygen in someone's blood. A normal, healthy human has a pulse oximeter reading above 95% when breathing normal atmospheric air ("room air"). We placed the sensor on Linda's finger and waited for the measurement to display. It was 38%.

I was already in the process of opening an oxygen mask before the number showed up on the screen but was taken aback by how low it was. She technically needed to have someone assist her ventilations with a bag-valve-mask. By using the BVM we would be able to force a greater volume of air into her chest and improve both her oxygenation and ventilation. It was then that I realized that I may just end up having to intubate her.

As we moved her to the stretcher I asked my dad if she had been sick recently. He said that she was up most of the night vomiting and had left the bedroom at some point to lay on the couch. He found her this morning when he woke up and came out into the living room so it's not really known how long she was in that condition. Much longer and things may have been <u>much</u> worse by the time we got there.

In the back of the ambulance we quickly performed a physical exam, obtained an ECG of her heart, and started an IV. Her blood pressure was low and her heart rate was slightly elevated. She was on multiple medications for pain, including narcotics, and the thought went through my head that perhaps she had accidentally overdosed.

I reached for the anti-narcotic medication, naloxone, and administered it through her IV. But there was no improvement in her condition. Her respiratory effort did not improve, and her level of consciousness remained severely depressed. With the oxygen mask her pulse oximeter levels only increased to the mid-80s. There was no more avoiding it; I had to intubate her.

We called for an additional ambulance to come to the scene so we could have someone there to drive us to the hospital. Given the condition of the patient there would need to be at least two of us in the back of the ambulance. It's not like working in an ER where you can have an entire group of people in one room to work on a critical patient. Out here, sometimes it's just you, your partner, and the patient.

I reached for my airway kit and removed the equipment that I would need to perform the intubation. I then removed the sedation and paralytic medications from the medication box and drew up the appropriate dosages, based on her estimated weight. It was then that I started to get nervous.

As discussed earlier, the procedure we use to intubate a patient who is spontaneously breathing is called Rapid Sequence Intubation (RSI). It involves completely paralyzing a patient, which loosens their jaw muscles and facilitates the passing of the breathing tube (called an endotracheal tube) through the patient's vocal cords and into their windpipe. But by paralyzing them you also take away their ability to breathe on their own. In this particular case, Linda wasn't breathing well, but she was breathing. Once I push that medication she will stop breathing on her own and we will be 100% responsible for her breathing. If we mess up, if I mess up, her heart will stop due to a lack of oxygen. It's been known to happen. Complications could include failing to get a good mask seal with the BVM and providing inefficient breaths, or I could accidentally pass the tube into her esophagus instead of her windpipe, or not be able to see her vocal cords at all. Based on my experience, I did not anticipate a difficult intubation based on her external anatomy, but sometimes the internal anatomy can surprise you once you're in there.

Ashlee could tell I was hesitant.

"Let's just wait on the other truck to get here," she said.

The second ambulance was also a paramedic unit so there would be another medic available to do the procedure once they got there; EMTs are not trained or authorized to do it in our state.

"No. It needs to be done," I said.

I pushed the sedative drug first. Even though she was unconscious it's always a good idea to give sedation because you never know if someone might wake up after you paralyze them. The last thing you want anyone to go through is being awake while paralyzed.

After the sedative was administered I followed it up with the paralytic. We used the BVM to "bag" her until her pulse oximeter measurement was in the high 90s, this is simply termed pre-oxygenation and removes nitrogen from the lungs creating an oxygen-rich environment for the procedure. After a short while pre-oxygenating her, I removed the bag and placed the laryngoscope into her mouth. I leaned down to look into her throat and was pleasantly surprised to see her vocal cords without any difficulty. I passed the tube, inflated the cuff, and connected the BVM to the tube.

We squeezed the bag to deliver oxygen directly down the tube and into her lungs. I listened to her chest on both sides and confirmed that there was good air movement. After using other methods we have available to us to ensure the tube was in the correct place I secured it to prevent it from becoming dislodged. I let out a huge sigh of relief, looked at Ashlee and smiled, and then looked out the back window of our ambulance to see the other ambulance pulling up behind us.

The other crew opened up the back doors to our truck.

"What can we do to help?" they asked.

I asked the paramedic to ride with me in the back of my ambulance while Ashlee drove us to the hospital. She was happy to oblige. On the way to the hospital she helped me monitor Linda and make sure she remained stable. Her oxygen levels remained at 98-100%, and her skin color returned to the pink complexion it normally should be.

I called in the radio report to the hospital to let them know what we were bringing, just like I had done hundreds, if not thousands, of times before. But this time I found my voice to be a little shaky. There were no changes in her condition during the five minute trip to the hospital. We had managed to stabilize her. We arrived in the ambulance bay and unloaded the stretcher.

"This is my step-mother so treat her like family," I said as we rolled the stretcher into the trauma room.

I proceeded to give a verbal report to the nurse who would be the primary caregiver for Linda. That's when I looked up to see the doctor walk into the trauma room and I had never felt more relieved during this call than I did at the very moment.

The physician who came in to take care of her was Dr. James Milstead. Dr. Milstead was nothing short of a mentor to me. I had known him my entire career and had learned so much from him during my years in EMS.

"What do you have, Chris?" Dr. Milstead asked.

I stepped over to him and began to fill him in, knowing that Linda was in the best hands possible.

*   *   *

Dr. Milstead was easy to look up to. He was smart, kind, and respectful. He was one of the few doctors who you never felt looked down at you simply because you were an EMT or paramedic. He was always available to answer questions you might have about an interesting run and provide some tips and tricks that he had stored in his head after years of service. Even if you messed up on something, he was not the kind of person to berate or belittle you. Instead, he would take the situation and turn it into a learning experience.

When I was applying for admission into a Critical Care Transport training program Dr. Milstead wrote a touching letter of recommendation for me and to my surprise also submitted a nomination letter for the NAEMT National Awards of Excellence Paramedic of The Year award. To this day I keep copies of those letters.

On more than one occasion Dr. Milstead treated my father (who has a long history of heart problems) in the very emergency department that I took Linda to that day. One particular visit to the ER that I remember was when my dad went in with chest pain. I walked over to the doctor's office area to see who was working. I was glad to see that one of the docs that was on was Dr. Milstead.

I went up to him and asked, "Do you have a big patient load right now?"

With a bit of a sigh he responded, "Oh yeah. Why, what's up?"

"My father just came in with chest pain," I explained.

"What room is he in?" he responded without hesitation. That simple question in and of itself spoke volumes to me about the kind of man he was.

There was even once he stood up for me to a new ER resident that I was butting heads with over a patient that I brought in. The best part of that whole event was I was actually right (thank God)! I remember Dr. Milstead looking at me from his corner computer station and giving me a sly wink when it was revealed that I was in fact correct for making the decision I did when it came to treating that patient.

Dr. Milstead had served in the United States Air Force during Vietnam. He was an active member in his church. He was the medical director of the nation's only charity air medical ambulance service, Grace on Wings, and was also Chairman of the Board of Directors for Hope in the Harvest Missions International, a non-profit organization which operated in Liberia. Amazingly, he also had time to be a published author of two books.

In the fall of 2015 I brought a patient into the local ER and noticed that there was a "Get Well" card laying on the counter at the nurse's station. I asked the secretary on duty, Maggie, who it was for.

"You haven't heard?" she asked. The look on my face must've given a clear answer because she continued without me answering.

"Dr. Milstead has cancer."

I was speechless. The only other time in my life when I was truly speechless was when I found out my wife was pregnant. This was a different type of speechless. I was suddenly consumed with feelings of sadness and anger. She went on to explain that it was a rare, fairly aggressive type of cancer. I had no words. There were no words that could be spoken. Everyone in this line of work ends up having a mentor whether they mean to or not, and I just found out that the man that had been mine for the last decade was very sick.

Dr. Milstead and I were "friends" on one of my social media accounts so I would occasionally see updates posted on his page. From time to time it seemed as if things might be going in the right direction. More than once I considered writing him an email to tell him how much I appreciated everything he taught me through the years and for always being there for me professionally. But I couldn't bring myself to do it. It seemed too "doom and gloom" to me. I would soon regret not doing it.

On the morning of March 11, 2016 I woke up and did my usual routine of browsing my social media page to see what kinds of things I missed happening overnight. On this particular morning I was shocked and saddened to see a post announcing the passing of Dr. Milstead, who had died at his residence surrounded by family. Almost immediately, I felt something that I hadn't felt in a very, very long time. It was a tear running down my cheek. I immediately thought about the last conversation I had with him.

It was the day after I had brought in a victim from a serious car accident. The man suffered a significant head injury after being ejected from his car. While we were en route to the hospital I requested that a medical helicopter be started for the hospital because I knew this patient would need to be transported to a trauma center. Sure enough, he was transported shortly after our arrival at the ER.

That next morning, Dr. Milstead stopped me when I came in to tell me that the patient had suffered a traumatic brain injury and that it was a good call on my part to have the helicopter started to the ER before we got there. It wasn't that big of a deal because that's just part of the job, but that's the kind of guy he was, always willing to give a little kudos where he thought it was due.

"Want to do it again today?" I said jokingly.

He cocked his head, smiled, and said "Or not."

He turned to walk back to his computer station.

"Have a good day, Chris," he said.

"You too, doc," I said through a laugh as I turned to walk back out to the ambulance.

And that would be the last conversation I ever had with him. For all of the things that he taught me, for all of the times that he treated my father, and for taking care of Linda (who is alive and well today), I will forever be grateful for having known him.

This job is too stressful, too demanding, to not have someone you can turn to when you need to vent, bounce an idea around with, or just talk to about something no one else will ever understand. And it's important that whomever that person is knows what they mean to you.

You may lose your chance to tell them.

- 9 -

The Other Four-Letter Word

It was a chilly morning in late Fall. The shift started off like any other. My partner and I received report from the off-going crew, checked the inventory, oxygen, and gas level on the truck and then stopped at the local donut shop for breakfast; something we did almost every shift.

Once we were back at the firehouse and our breakfast had been consumed, I was in the process of cleaning the back of the ambulance when our tones went off. The call was for a cardiac arrest in the northern area of our response district. We jumped in the cab of the truck, pulled out of the bay, and marked en route to the scene.

"Clear," dispatch acknowledged us on the radio. "Be advised, this will be an 11-year old male. Unresponsive. Not breathing."

I looked at my partner, but no words had to be exchanged.

I immediately started forming a plan in my head. What size IV was I going to use? What dosing of medications was indicated? What size endotracheal tube does the average 11-year old require? Everything changes when it's a kid. The numbers aren't so "cookbook" in nature. You've got to use your head. You have to do some medication math. Not to mention, I was wondering what would've caused an 11-year old to go into cardiac arrest.

Did they have some kind of congenital heart condition? Was it a drowning? Was it some kind of traumatic injury? Most likely it was respiratory related. One of the most common causes of cardiac arrest in children is respiratory failure. The heart succumbs to a lack of oxygen due to whatever the respiratory malfunction is and stops beating. But that usually applies to younger children. Whatever the cause, time was of the essence. Brain cells begin to die 4-6 minutes after the heart stops and oxygen supply is interrupted.

We were going fast; really fast. But we were also being careful knowing that if we crashed, hurting ourselves or someone else, that it did no good for the patient on scene or anyone else. A deputy from the sheriff's office ended up right behind us at one point, heading to the same location we were. Another deputy was en route as well, and members of the local volunteer fire department were also responding. Everybody was coming as fast as we could.

We heard the fire department's rescue squad mark on the scene when we were about two minutes out. We pulled up to the house and started backing up the driveway. We had made it there in eight minutes. I wasn't even out of the ambulance yet and I could hear it: the unmistakable loud cries from the patient's mother.

"Hurry!" she yelled through tears. "He's not breathing!"

It's a gut-wrenching sound, one that sticks in your head for days following a call like that. At that point I knew this was the real deal. There was no miscommunication with dispatch. They hadn't misinterpreted something the caller was telling them during the 911 call. This was real. We were going to walk into this house and find a dead kid.

I shifted the truck into park, my partner and I jumped out, grabbed our equipment and made our way into the house. I didn't run, but I walked a lot faster than I normally do. I made it a point a long time ago to never run on a scene. It's dangerous to run on a scene in my opinion. Even the time that it was my own step-mother I didn't run. You have to maintain your composure on these scenes. Running just gets your heart rate up and your adrenaline rushing, and that's not what I need in a situation like this.

My partner was a few steps ahead of me as we entered the house. The patient's older brother, a teenager, directed us to a bedroom straight back from the front door. As I approached, I could see a lifeless blue body on the ground. Two firefighters were performing CPR.

I remember thinking to myself how small the boy looked for an 11-year old. He was about the same size as my 6-year old. I made it a point not to look at his face. I often did that with my pediatric arrests.

Don't look at them.

Don't personalize it.

Stay focused. Do your job.

Over the years I had unwillingly developed a reputation for being particularly skilled when it came to handling pediatric emergencies in the out-of-hospital environment. Sadly, I became quite comfortable with these types of calls because for some reason I seemed to get them quite often. I considered it a blessing and a curse. On one hand, my continued exposure to these emergencies had eventually allowed me to become quite comfortable with handling them, but on the other hand I was only comfortable because I had the misfortune of responding to so many. And here we were again.

My partner immediately removed our defibrillation and monitoring pads from the cardiac monitor and placed them on the child's chest so we could see what type of cardiac rhythm he had. As expected, the rhythm displayed on the monitor was asystole – a flat line. It would be unusual to find a pediatric patient in a shockable rhythm. Asystole is not considered a shockable rhythm; there is nothing electrical therapy can do. At this point the only thing we could provide was good chest compressions and airway management, consisting of oxygenation and ventilation, along with some IV fluids and medications.

I quickly opened my airway kit, removed the laryngoscope and endotracheal tube, got down on my belly, tilted the boy's head back, inserted the laryngoscope into his mouth, and visualized his vocal cords. It was an easy intubation. His vocal cords were easy to visualize and the tube went in without difficulty.

All the while, the child's mother was understandably screaming and crying while she watched us performing CPR on her son. She was standing just outside the room as her older son paced anxiously in the background. Although I completely understood her current emotional state, and sympathized with her, she was being too much of a distraction, and so I asked one of the deputies to take her outside and find out what they could about what happened and about the boy's medical history.

It turns out that the patient had a history of asthma and had developed some shortness of breath after waking up. He attempted to use his inhaler but his condition did not improve. Realizing the gravity of the situation his mother called 911, and while she was on the phone with the 911 dispatcher her son collapsed and stopped breathing. The family was directed to begin CPR while waiting on first responders to arrive.

As we continued to work on the boy, I placed an IV in his external jugular vein on the left side of his neck. The "EJ," as we call them, came to be my go-to for venous access in a cardiac arrest situation. I preferred it because of the simple fact that it essentially

130

emptied directly into the heart thus providing a direct route for medications to travel.

I immediately administered a dose of epinephrine. In this particular case the EPI would serve two purposes: it would directly affect the heart in an attempt to restart it, but it would also work to open up the child's airways which had constricted during his asthma attack. After the breathing tube was put in, we had noticed that his lung sounds were very diminished and even squeezing the bag-valve-mask was difficult due to the amount of resistance in his airways. His exhaled carbon dioxide levels were also noted to be nearly 80mmhg, a clear indication of what had precipitated this event.

What a lot of people don't understand about asthma is that it's not a breathing in problem; it's a breathing *out* problem. As a patient's lower airways constrict, CO_2 becomes trapped, the patient is unable to exhale, and a vicious cycle ensues. If it is not reversed quickly the patient experiences respiratory failure followed closely by respiratory arrest and then full cardiac arrest. And this is exactly what had happened this morning.

The first round of epinephrine did not result in any immediate change in the patient's condition. We continued doing high-quality chest compressions and ventilating the patient through the breathing tube. His color was improving slightly, and when the time came, I pushed a second dose of epinephrine. A few seconds later I glanced at the monitor screen and something caught my eye. Mixed in with all of the motion artifact there appeared to be some type of organized rhythm.

"Stop compressions," I ordered.

The firefighter doing compressions lifted his hands off of the boy's chest. The motion artifact displayed on the monitor screen, caused by the chest compressions, dissipated to reveal what appeared to be a normal cardiac rhythm. I quickly took my stethoscope and placed it on the boy's chest above his heart.

"Everybody quiet," I said as I listened closely.

And there it was, faint at first and then increasingly louder and louder and louder: his heartbeat had returned.

"He's got a heartbeat," I said.

"Yes!" exclaimed one of the firefighters.

The boy's mother, still in the front room, heard the firefighter's exuberant outburst. "Is he breathing?!" she asked.

"No, he's not breathing," I answered honestly. "But his heart is beating on its own and right now that's the most important thing. We can breathe for him."

She started crying hysterically again, overwhelmed with a mixture of fear, hope, sadness, and God only knows what else. I leaned over and checked the boy's pupils: non-reactive.

Shit.

His pupils being non-reactive was a bad sign; although, it was not a surprising discovery. His brain had been deprived of oxygen for an extended period of time. Even though we got his heart going again, it would take a miracle for him to pull through unscathed. *A big miracle.*

We checked his blood pressure, blood glucose, and ECG. All were essentially normal. His lung sounds were improving and he was moving air much better. For all intents and purposes he had made a major turn for the positive, but he was far from out of the woods. He would need a Pediatric Intensive Care Unit (PICU) – a service not provided at any of the local hospitals. The closest PICU was about 90 minutes from our current location.

"Steve, I need a favor," I said as I turned to one of the deputies. "Get on with dispatch and have them start a helicopter to meet us at the hospital."

"You got it," Steve replied.

The goal would be to transport the boy to the hospital, meet the helicopter at the helipad and have them fly him to the children's hospital located about 80 miles away.

"Is he going to be OK?" the mother asked.

Years of experience told me that the answer was "no," but he had made it this far so you never truly know until you know. I turned and looked at her and said, "He's stable for the moment, but he is still very critical."

I explained the plan when it came to transporting him to the children's hospital. We then packaged him onto a backboard and carried him to our stretcher which had been placed outside the front door. After loading him into the ambulance we began the fifteen minute trip to the hospital.

While in transit, I started a second IV line, gave him some IV fluids, and monitored his cardiac rhythm and vital signs. His skin condition had improved dramatically. He was warm and pink now. Normal. His oxygen levels had returned to normal levels and with very purposeful and specific ventilation techniques, we had successfully decreased his CO_2 measurements to near-normal levels.

He took a few breaths on his own and appeared to gag a little on the breathing tube; good signs, but he was still completely unresponsive and his pupils were still non-reactive. We watched him closely. His vitals remained stable, and for the duration of the transport there weren't any other significant changes.

We knew there was a helicopter on the way to meet us at the hospital but due to radio incompatibilities between us and them we were unable to make direct contact. As we arrived at the hospital, we noted that the ground helipad was empty; they had not arrived yet, and we didn't see them anywhere overhead.

Not knowing how far out they were I decided to go ahead and take the patient inside the ER. I'd rather have him in there where we'd have some additional help than sitting in the back of my ambulance for an undetermined amount of time waiting on the aircraft to arrive.

We drove around to the ambulance entrance of the ER and parked. My partner jumped out and began to unload the stretcher as the patient's mother walked up.

She had been in a van that was following us all the way to the hospital. Despite the fact that we had our lights and sirens on while we were transporting, she was on our tail the entire way, caution lights flashing on their vehicle. At one point we came to a red light and had to stop to clear the intersection before continuing; they honked. To this day we're not sure if they were honking at us because we had stopped or if they were honking at cross traffic. It wasn't the safest decision they made to ride our bumper the whole way in, but I get it.

"Can I go in with you?" she asked as we prepared to walk in the ER.

"Yes," I said. "But you have to try and stay calm so these guys can do their jobs."

We walked in and were greeted with expressions of confusion. After all, when we called in our radio report we had told them that we would be meeting the air medical crew at the ground pad. They weren't expecting us to be coming into the ER.

"Rapid response to Peds Trauma," the unit secretary announced over the intercom system. "Dr. Holmes to Peds Trauma."

As we walked into the pediatric trauma room, one of the ER nurses approached us.

"They're landing on the roof right now," she said.

"We didn't know where they were," I said. "We didn't have any radio contact with them and didn't see them out there. I had no idea how far out they were."

Dr. Holmes, one of the ER physicians and the EMS Medical Director, walked into the room.

"What do you want us to do, Doc?" I asked.

"There's really not much else for us to do," she said. "You guys have done all the hard work."

"Do you want us to go ahead and take him up?"

She leaned over and glanced at the monitor to review his vital signs. They had remained stable.

"Yeah. Go ahead and take him up."

A security guard and one of the ER nurses joined us as we walked down the hallways that led to the elevator. We got on and went upstairs to the fourth floor where access to the rooftop helipad was. We exited the elevator, turned the corner, and approached the ramp that led outside. At the same time, the flight crew was walking into the building with their stretcher.

"We can't take him," the flight nurse said.

"What do you mean?" I asked.

"He's been in the hospital, he has to be seen in the ER."

She was referring to a requirement that once a patient enters the hospital they must be assessed by a physician and then a transfer between facilities must be officially requested and carried out. At this point it would be an additional delay in definitive care, all in the name of red tape.

"Come on guys, he's an 11 year old kid," the firefighter that had drove us in and gone upstairs with us said in frustration.

"I'll have to call my supervisor," the flight nurse advised before stepping off to the side, pulling out her cellphone, and making the call.

By this time we had started to attract a group of onlookers. Hospital staff members, visitors, and even a group of nursing students who had just exited another set of elevators were all watching us. After a moment the flight nurse hung up her phone and walked back over to us.

"Tony says to do what's in the best interest of the patient and we'll figure everything else out later."

Smart move, Tony.

We were finally free to transfer the young boy to their care. We carefully moved him over to their stretcher. We disconnected him from our equipment and hooked him up to theirs. I gave them a report about what happened, what we did, and how he responded to our treatment. At that point they wheeled him away, loaded him into their helicopter, and departed.

Typically that would be the end of it for me. We'd go back to our ambulance, clean up, restock, and then I'd finish up the paperwork, but that wasn't the case this time. This time I *had* to know what the outcome was going to be. I couldn't just let this one go. No way.

In all the years that I had been doing this job I had done CPR on way too many kids and unfortunately in every single case they died, despite our best efforts and the efforts of the hospital's staff. But this time was different. This time we got him back. His heart was beating. He had a blood pressure. He was even taking a few breaths on his own. These were all good signs and I could feel it inside me. I could feel the one thing that I tell people not to hold onto too tightly in these situations. Something I began to refer to as "the other four-letter word."

I had hope.

The Good Fight

I stood in the shower as the water poured over my head. The last bit of warm water was beginning to dissipate, slowly turning colder and colder with each drop. I had been in there for easily half an hour just thinking. Thinking about whether there was anything that we could've done differently. Better. Faster. *Anything.*

It had been a week since responding to Hayden's house. A week since his mother, sobbing and wailing from a pain like no other, begged us to save her son. A week since we worked to bring him back from the dead. A senseless cardiac arrest resulting from an extreme asthma attack. Our hard work had somewhat paid off; we did get his heart beating again. I even saw him take some breaths on his own in the back of my ambulance, before loading him into the helicopter which flew him to the children's hospital.

But that was a week ago. A lot can happen in a week. It turned out that Hayden's father and I had a mutual friend and through him I was able to stay updated on the boy's progress. Unfortunately, it was not good news.

Radiographic scans showed damage to his brain, he began to have seizures and issues keeping his body temperature regulated. The doctors and nurses fought for days to improve his prognosis to no avail. His parents made the gut-wrenching decision to remove him from life support, and he died a short time later.

The news was not surprising to me. Years of experience and training told me exactly what the outcome was going to be, but nevertheless, like I said, I had hope. I'm not sure what it was about this particular call that made it so different. Maybe it was the fact that although he was several years older than my son, there were some similarities between them. Or maybe it was simply sympathizing with his mother. Regardless, I let my guard down.

Over the next several days, I debated whether or not I would go to his funeral. The thought had never crossed my mind for any previous patients, so I spoke to my partner about it and came to the conclusion that it would be inappropriate of me to do so. It turned out the funeral was scheduled for one of our shift days anyway, so that helped.

I spent several days going through the call over and over again in my head. I read the run sheet a dozen times. I couldn't help but wonder if there was anything that I could have done differently. And that's exactly what I was thinking as I stood in the shower as the cold water started to make me shiver. The rapid chill brought me back to my senses. I shut the water off, grabbed a towel, stepped out of the shower, and dried off.

As I wiped the mirror clear and looked into the eyes of my own reflection, the truth of the situation was clear.

There's nothing else you could've done.

Our response to the scene was rapid. Our treatment was timely and precise. Every decision we made was correct. It just wasn't enough. The damage was done. Some people might say, "God had other plans for him." Well, whatever the reason, he was dead, and it was time to move on from it. But it being Christmas Eve made it a little harder to do that. Seeing my own son enjoying school break and the perks of the holidays made it a little harder to do that. And there was one other thing that I had to do before I could lock this call into that little box in the back of my head.

*   *   *

It was a miserable Christmas Eve day. Overcast. Cold. Wet. No snow. Just rain. I pulled through the gates at the entrance of the cemetery and made my way back to where my friend had told me Hayden's gravesite was. I parked my truck and made my way through the grass to find his headstone. It took me a minute, but I was finally able to locate it.

It looked brand new. I'm not sure how long it had actually been in place. I don't really know how long it takes to get one of those made. Hopefully, it's not something I'll have to personally find out for a long time to come. I looked down and read it, focusing on the "born" and "death" dates. He was less than 5 months away from his 12th birthday. I shook my head. My attention then focused on the hyphen between those dates, and it made me think of something I had heard on a radio show once.

A caller had dialed in to speak on a talk radio show and mentioned that we have the date of our birth, the date of our death, and a "small little dash that represents everything that happens between the two." That "little dash" represents so much: the first smile, the first laugh, first steps, first kiss, first love, and so much more. A lifetime of experiences and memories is encapsulated in that small, little dash. And as I stared down at it, as the rain began to fall again, I had a sudden moment of clarity.

You see, for the first time in my career I had been thinking about quitting; getting out of the business of life and death. Finding something different to do that would not weigh so heavily on my mind and soul. But that day, standing in the cemetery, looking at that hyphen

140

engraved on that headstone, made me think of a quote that I heard on a TV show but had long since forgotten.

It was an episode of the TV show *ER,* and the character of Dr. Carter was speaking to a medical student whose patient had died and was attempting to offer her some reassurance.

"Some patients get to you more than others, I know," he said. "But when you've done everything you can, even more than you thought you could, you have to go on knowing you fought the good fight."

Truer words have never been spoken and for them to pop into my head after what was surely years and years since seeing the episode was hard for me to explain. But, nonetheless, it was exactly what I needed. Suddenly my mind shifted to thinking about the names and faces of those who wouldn't be alive if it hadn't been for me, my partner, and the other first responders who answered their call for help.

It was then that I felt something I hadn't felt for a few weeks. Relief. I felt relieved. A small smile even made its way across my face. I knelt down and placed my hand onto the headstone.

"Thank you."

I stood up and turned to walk back towards my truck, with almost a feeling of being revitalized. Some people spend their whole lives trying to figure out what they're meant to do, but in that moment I knew that how I've spent my life is exactly how I was meant to spend it.

Fighting the good fight.

-AFTERWORD-

S quad 81, Medic 89, Squad 1, 9339 N. Crescent Point Lane, cardiac arrest."

We had just pulled into the parking lot of a local restaurant to get lunch when the call came out over the radio, once again showing Murphy's Law of EMS in action. My partner Nick and I had been trying to get a meal break in for a few hours, but it obviously wasn't going to be happening anytime soon. I turned the truck around and drove towards the exit of the parking lot, flipping the lights and sirens on.

"89's responding," I said over the radio.

"Clear, 89. This is going to be a 77 year old male, face down on his bed, not breathing, unresponsive," the dispatcher relayed.

We weren't far from the residence. We arrived on scene in just over three minutes. As we were pulling up, a sheriff's deputy who had arrived just prior to us was walking up to the front door. I placed the ambulance in park, got out, and walked around to the side door of the patient compartment. Nick was in the back and handed off equipment to me.

As I entered the house, I was directed to a back bedroom. When I made entry into the bedroom, I saw two people kneeling down at the patient's side. He had been moved from the bed and placed on the floor. The bystanders, later identified as neighbors of the patient, were performing CPR. A man was providing chest compressions and a woman was holding the patient's airway open. She looked at me as soon as I walked in.

"He has agonal respirations and a very weak pulse," she said.

I think she could tell by my facial expression that I was a little surprised by her use of appropriate medical lingo.

"I'm a respiratory therapist," she said.

I sat the cardiac monitor on the bed just above the patient's location and removed the defibrillation pads. I cut off the patient's shirt and began applying the pads.

"What types of medical problems does he have?" I asked his wife, Cheryl, who was standing in the doorway watching.

"He just had a triple bypass a few months ago," Cheryl said, a fact proven by the appearance of the scar running up and down the center of his chest.

"Was he complaining of anything today?" I asked. "Chest pain? Shortness of breath? Anything?"

"No, nothing. We've been out shopping and we had lunch. We just got home a little while ago."

"Did you see him collapse?"

"No," Cheryl said. "We hadn't been home ten minutes and I found him lying on the bed."

I finished placing the pads on his chest and looked at the monitor's screen. The patient was in ventricular fibrillation, or v-fib. V-fib is a common rhythm seen in sudden cardiac arrest patients and needs immediate treatment with an electrical shock delivered from the monitor/defibrillator.

"He's in v-fib. Everybody stand clear," I said to the neighbors performing CPR.

As the monitor charged up to deliver the shock, Nick stepped around me and moved the neighbors clear of the patient.

"Thanks for your help, guys. We've got it from here," he said.

Once the monitor was charged, I verified that everyone was clear of the patient and then pressed the "shock" button. The patient's body jumped as the electricity was delivered. I continued chest compressions as Nick used a BVM to deliver breaths.

I looked over at the deputy who was standing nearby. "Can you do me a favor, man?" I asked. "Here in just a second, I need you to grab his ankles and pull him around the bed."

The patient, Harry, had been placed on the floor at the foot of the bed between the bed itself and a large dresser. There was only about two feet of space to work in so we needed to move him.

"Nick, grab his head."

"Yeah, I've got it."

"Okay, go ahead and pull," I said to the deputy.

We quickly moved Harry to the other side of the bed which allowed ample space to continue our resuscitation efforts. By this time, members of the local fire department were arriving.

Kendall and Brycen, two EMTs who also worked with me at the ambulance service, walked into the room.

"What do you need, Chris?" Kendall asked.

"Can you take over chest compressions so I can get him intubated?"

Kendall stepped over Harry's body and knelt down to take over chest compressions. I stepped around to his head and opened our jump kit to remove the intubation kit.

"Let's go ahead and check his rhythm," I said.

Compressions were stopped so we could review the rhythm displayed on the monitor screen. It was still v-fib.

"Charge it to 300," I said.

Brycen was standing next to the monitor and increased the energy setting to 300 joules before pressing the "charge" button. Once it was fully charged, the monitor began sounding the telltale alarm indicating it was ready to deliver a shock.

"Everybody clear," Brycen said. He then made sure that no one was touching the patient and delivered the shock.

"Resume chest compressions," I said.

Kendall continued doing chest compressions while I laid on my stomach to intubate Harry. I placed the laryngoscope into his mouth and lifted his jaw to view his vocal cords. His cords were quite anterior and difficult to see.

"Brycen, put your hand on his throat," I directed.

Brycen placed his fingers on Harry's throat and I used a technique referred to as ELM or external laryngeal manipulation. Basically, while I'm looking into the patient's mouth, I put my hands

145

on top of Brycen's and move the patient's external anatomy around to allow me better visualization of his vocal cords.

"Got them. Hold it right there."

I was able to see the cords finally and then passed the endotracheal tube through them. After confirming proper tube placement, we secured the tube in place and continued providing breaths.

Just then, Jarred, another paramedic on the fire department stepped into the room.

"What can I do?" he asked.

"Throw in a line," I replied and Jarred moved to the patient's side to find a vein for an IV.

I stood up and moved to the patient's feet so I could keep an eye on the big picture and the progress of the resuscitation.

"Alright, let's check his rhythm," I said.

Kendall stopped doing chest compressions as we all looked towards the monitor screen. The patient was still in v-fib.

"Charge it up," I said as Brycen pushed the charge button yet again before delivering another shock.

The patient's rhythm would try to convert to an organized rhythm after each shock but would quickly revert back to v-fib each time. Things weren't looking promising.

As Jarred inserted an IV into Harry's jugular vein, I used the IO drill to place a needle into the man's tibia. We used the access sites to administer IV fluids and medications designed to get Harry's heart pumping again and eliminate the arrhythmia.

For the next several minutes we continued providing chest compressions, artificial ventilations, IV medications, and additional shocks for the v-fib. After the seventh shock, we checked his rhythm again.

"Hold up, we've got an organized rhythm," I said. "Is there a pulse with that?"

Kendall reached for the patient's carotid pulse and placed his fingers against it. My eyes went back and forth from the monitor screen to Kendall's fingers as I waited until he finally commented.

"Yeah, he's got one. I've got a carotid."

"Someone verify, please," I requested.

Jarred was still sitting by Harry's head so he reached over and felt for a pulse to double-check Kendall's findings.

"Yep. He's got one," Jarred said.

"Good deal. Okay, let's get a 12-lead and a blood pressure," I said.

Kendall and Brycen worked to get the ECG and a blood pressure. Meanwhile, I looked at Josh and Zach, two of the firefighters on scene whom I had asked earlier to come up with a way to get Harry out of the house.

"We have an extraction plan?" I asked.

"Yeah. Cot's in place at the end of the hall. We'll have to carry him out to it though," Josh said.

Harry's blood pressure was surprisingly near normal. Brycen handed off the printed ECG to me. Not surprisingly, the ECG showed signs of oxygen deprivation to the heart. Suddenly, I heard the beeping sound of Harry's heart rate increasing. I looked toward the monitor to see that his rhythm had converted to ventricular tachycardia, or v-tach. V-tach can be just as dangerous as v-fib.

"He's in v-tach," I said. "Does he still have a pulse?"

Whether Harry had a pulse or not would determine the next step in treatment. Kendall reached for the carotid artery once again.

"Yeah, he's still got one," he said.

"Okay. We need to sync-cardiovert," I said. "Charge to 100."

Jarred reached over and pressed the "SYNC" switch on the monitor's control panel. By doing so, it will allow the monitor to deliver a shock at a very specific point in the conduction cycle of the heart. Once the monitor was ready and charged, the shock was delivered. Harry's body once again jumped. Fortunately, the v-tach was terminated and his heart returned to a normal rhythm.

"Okay guys, let's get him packaged up. I'm going to talk to the wife real quick," I said before stepping out of the bedroom and going down the hallway to the kitchen where Cheryl was waiting.

"Okay, we've got his heart beating again," I said.

"Thank God," Cheryl said, relieved. Although I could see the relief in her face and hear it in her voice, I had to make sure she understood the dire situation Harry was in. Only about 6% of out of hospital cardiac arrest patients survive.

"He's still in very critical condition," I said. "Basically what happened is his heart went into a chaotic rhythm so it wasn't able to beat appropriately. We had to shock him several times and give him medicine to make that rhythm break. Right now, we're breathing for him and he's still unconscious. There's a chance that this was caused by a blockage in one of his coronary arteries, but I can't say for sure if that's the case. The doctors will have to decide if he needs to go to the cath lab or not."

"Okay," Cheryl said. "Thank you so much."

"You're welcome," I said, but inside I knew that Harry's prognosis was poor. He had been down for nearly 20 minutes. Over the span of my career I've had dozens of cardiac arrests where we were able to get the heart beating again, but the patient's brain had been deprived of oxygen for too long, and they eventually died.

We loaded Harry into the ambulance, put him on a ventilator, started a continuous infusion of amiodarone in order to hopefully keep him from going back into v-fib or v-tach, and began transporting to the hospital. On the way there, Harry was breathing on his own but otherwise remained unresponsive. One promising sign was that his pupils reacted to light. It's not a definitive sign of a promising outcome; I'd seen it before in patients who ended up dying. We monitored him closely for changes, and there were none.

Once at the hospital, we turned him over to the ER team to let them do their thing. I walked out to the waiting room to fill the family in on how he did during the transport. They thanked me once again, and I wished them luck.

In my head I knew the truth. All we did was buy them some time to say goodbye.

149

The interesting thing about the case that you just read is that it happened after I received the original proof copy of this book. You see, the book originally ended with a different story, but when that call happened I decided to go back and change things. I suppose you could say it was almost fate that the call had occurred.

Now, you may be wondering why I feel it was fate that this call came just prior to finishing up this book. Well, allow me to explain it to you.

When I first entered this profession, my passion for it was fueled by adrenaline and heart-pounding calls like "cool" traumas. As time has gone on and I have aged and become wiser (hopefully), what drives me has changed. And this run reminded me of that.

It's not about the lights and sirens. It's not about those "cool" traumas. It's not about the procedures. It's about *helping people*. It's about being the one there for them when no one else is. Sometimes you show up and "save the day." And sometimes all you can do is offer a supportive hand on a shoulder. That's what it's really about.

*   *   *

Three days later...

We had just finished dropping off a patient at the ER, and I decided I wanted to check and see how Harry was doing. I didn't typically follow up on my cardiac arrest patients because their fate was usually sealed by the time we got them to the hospital. The brain just does not do well when it's deprived of oxygen, and after only a few minutes it begins to die. But the fact that Harry's pupils had been responsive and he had been breathing on his own gave me some hope. And as much as I despise that word after having been let down so many times, there was something different about this case.

I walked down to the hospital's EMS Coordinator's office and asked him to look up the patient and see if I could get an update. He typed in Harry's name and brought up his chart. As we looked over the assessment and progress notes I couldn't believe what I was reading:

> *Patient awake and following commands. Still on vent. Will remove from vent today.*

"Are you kidding me?" I asked. "When was that put in?"

The coordinator looked at the timestamp on the chart.

"Like three hours ago," he said.

"Unbelievable," I said.

"Sounds promising," he replied.

I got his room number and decided to go upstairs and check on him; see it with my own eyes. I was not working with Nick that day like I had been when we actually responded on Harry, but my partner AJ went up to the ICU with me.

As we rode the elevator up, I was still having a hard time believing it.

"Things sound promising," I said, echoing the EMS Coordinator.

"For sure," AJ replied.

We made it to the second floor, where the ICU was located, and stepped off the elevator. As luck would have it, as soon as I rounded the corner I saw Harry's wife in the hallway.

"Cheryl…" I said.

Cheryl turned and looked at me. It took a brief moment for her to recognize who I was but then a smile crossed her face.

"I was just coming up to check on him. How's he doing?" I asked as I walked up to her.

As soon as I was in range, Cheryl opened her arms to give me a hug.

"You saved his life," she said.

I leaned over and hugged her. I can't remember the last time I was given a hug that tight.

"So how is he?" I asked.

"Come with me," she said.

We walked around the corner and down the hall until we made it to Harry's room. Cheryl led the way into the room, and as she pulled the curtain back I couldn't believe what I saw.

Harry. Sitting up in bed, off the ventilator, wide awake.

"Harry," Cheryl said. "You probably don't remember these guys, but they're the ones that saved your life."

As technically true as that comment was, it still seemed not quite right to hear it spoken. We were just doing our job. I was curious to see how Harry responded. It would be a good indication of any brain damage he sustained. He looked over at us.

"You were there?" he asked.

"Yes, sir. Harry, you gave your wife quite a scare," I said.

As I stood there talking to him, I couldn't believe it. In 17 years of service, I had only had one other patient whom I had treated for cardiac arrest survive to hospital discharge, and that patient arrested right in front of me which increased his odds for survival. The fact that I was standing in that hospital room talking to a man who had been dead on the floor of his bedroom for twenty minutes was nothing short of amazing to me. Of all the things that I had experienced in my career, of all the patients I had treated, of all the lives that had been lost along the way, this moment was defining. It was a reminder to me of why I do what I do. A reminder of why EMS providers across the world serve their communities.

I talked with Harry and Cheryl for a few moments before shaking Harry's hand, hugging Cheryl one last time, and wishing them good luck. As I walked out of the room, I looked back at Cheryl sitting next to Harry, holding his hand. No further affirmation would ever be needed to remind me why I do what I do.

So, do you want to be a paramedic? Or know someone who is? Because that's the reality of it. It's not like on TV or in the movies. It's raw. It's real. It's blood, sweat, and tears. It's death and dying. It's mothers crying for their babies. It's knowing that sometimes you will save a life while other times you can only be there as someone grieves. It's soul-crushing. It's life-changing.

And it's completely worth it.

- About The Author -

J. Christopher Thomas is a seasoned paramedic, board-certified in flight paramedicine by the International Board of Specialty Certifications. Additionally, he is nationally registered as a paramedic by the National Registry of Emergency Medical Technicians and is also nationally certified as an EMS Educator by the National Association of EMS Educators.

Chris holds a bachelor's degree in business and has worked for nearly 20 years in the public service fields (fire, EMS, law enforcement); however, he has always found EMS to be his true passion.

His dedication to the profession and his patients has earned him multiple awards and citations including the Indiana Paramedic of the Year Award, Indiana EMS Primary Instructor of the Year Award, and Indiana EMS for Children Award.